# My Breakaway

Renee E Pitt

**Copyright © 2016 Renee E Pitt**

All rights reserved. No part of this publication may be reproduced, distributed or transmitted in any form or by any means, without prior written permission.

**National Library of Australia Cataloguing-in-Publication entry:**

Creator: Pitt, Renee E., author.
Title: My breakaway / Renee E Pitt.
ISBN: 9780994497703 (paperback)
ISBN: 9780994497710 (ebook)
Subjects: Pitt, Renee E.
Female offenders--Western Australia--Biography.
Drug addiction--Western Australia.
Life change events.
Inspiration.
Dewey Number: 364.374092

Cover photo: Emily Crewe
Cover layout: Pickawoowoo Publishing Group
Book Layout:© 2014 BookDesignTemplates.com
Publishing Consultants: Pickawoowoo Publishing Group

**Disclaimer**

Every intention has been kept to retain the authors voice in this biography. Her writing style, a combination of idiotypical usage of syntax, diction, punctuation, dialog, etc., within the body of text is unique and raw and conveys the author's attitude, personality, and character. The content is the important message and we encourage you to peruse accordingly. The views and opinions expressed in the work are solely those of the author. Some names may have been changed to protect privacy however they reflect real people and events.

# Dedication

*This book is in memory of the love of my life, Jerremy Wayde Kennedy, the man with whom I shared 13 years of my life and father of 11 children, who passed away suddenly on April 3, 2014.*

*I love you with all my heart Jer.*

*Your past doesn't always have to hold you back. You can learn from it, gain strength from it and then use it to move forward.*

*It won't happen overnight but with commitment, determination and resolve, you can succeed.*

*But the key is, believe in yourself and know that you are worth so much more.*

*Never give up. There is always a way.*

# Preface

Just before anyone reads this story, I would like to point out that everything I did was by my own choice. I was never forced or encouraged into any of my doings or actions. Each and every decision was made by me.

Some names have been changed.

This is written as I remember.

There will be some obscene language in this book but it is not said in any malice, this is just how we spoke.

This book is written by Renee Pitt, with a message to anyone who happens to find themselves in the drug scene, no matter how deep you feel you are in, there is a way out.

My story will show how easily anyone can fall into an addiction to risky behaviours without even realising it.

If I can get out of everything and off drugs after 23 years of addiction to risky behaviours – and an 18-year addiction to methamphetamines, then others can too.

# CONTENTS

My Early Years ................................................................................ 1
My First Criminal Charges ............................................................. 6
New Chance at Roadhouse Work ................................................. 17
Pregnant with Summer .................................................................. 23
New Job Opportunities .................................................................. 27
Back in Prison ............................................................................... 36
Meeting Jer .................................................................................... 44
Arrival of Children ........................................................................ 47
First Attempt at Trying to Get Off ................................................ 55
Funniest Day Ever – Jers Sarcasm ................................................ 59
In Prison Again ............................................................................. 64
Confronting My Dad ..................................................................... 72
Loosing Jer .................................................................................... 75

CHAPTER ONE

# My Early Years

During my younger life I would have been about seven when I realised I was adopted. No one ever told me, I think I just worked it out. My grandmother Barbara had actually adopted me when I was a baby and brought me out of hospital. She has been there since day one, so she is my mum.

As for my biological mother, I don't even know how I worked out who she was. I think she only came up to see mum about four times that I remember in my younger years. She used to come to talk to mum at the end of our driveway and talk with her for about ten minutes then leave. I knew she felt uncomfortable when speaking to me, but I didn't know why. It would be years until I found out her reason for this.

The person who was meant to be one of my big brothers, Darren, who worked in the North Sea as a deep-sea diver, used to come back to Australia every second or third Christmas for a couple of weeks at a time. He only used to spend time with me. I knew he was my dad, but I only ever called him by his name. These visits only lasted until I was about ten when he remarried in Aberdeen, Scotland, and he and his new wife had a baby girl.

At the age of thirteen he flew me over to come to stay with him and his new family for a couple of months. Darren was away on the rigs for the first four weeks, so I spent the time with his wife, Jenni, and my half-sister, Victoria. It was good to get to know them but finally at the end of January, 1990, Darren came home. We went up to the local artificial ski ramp, which is basically just a big piece of mesh foam, so I could learn to ski. Once he thought I had a bit of an idea what to do we all went up to the Lecht Ski Resort to give it a go. This time it was on real snow so there was a massive difference, but it was all fun anyway. We made our way up to the top of the slopes, then my dad went down first and got his video camera out. I remember thinking, "wow man, this looks so steep", but I was pretty adventurous so I thought I'd give it a go, and down I went…I hit the first mogul, which is a bump on a ski slope, and that was it, I started tumbling like you would not believe. One ski went this way and the other went the other way. My dad was laughing so hard – and when I stopped, so was I. I will never forget this trip even though we only had a few days to spend together before it was time for me to head back home to Australia and before my dad had to go back to work on the rigs, so we made the most of the few days we had. We caught a bus from Aberdeen down to Edinburgh to stay a night with Jenni's brother and his family. While we were there we did the tour through Edinburgh Castle. We also went to the Military Museum – I don't really remember that much about this place but I do remember I had a smile on my face that was absolutely priceless. Then the next morning we were on the bus again to head down to London. While we were there we went to Madame Tussauds Wax Museum. This place was exceptional, the sculptures looking so much like the real people. I had my photo taken with Mr T who I thought was so cool, as did any thirteen-year-old back then. I had my photo taken with the Royal Family, Michael Jackson and so many others. There was one part of the museum I remember so well, it was called the horror room. I have to say this place absolutely spooked me, there were villains, serial murderers, executioners and their victims. It showed so much horrific history from the past five centuries.

The next morning it was time to head to the airport for my flight home. Even though I spent only a short time with dad I honestly thought we had actually started to build a father-daughter relationship for the first time in my life. I thought we would continue this way even after my return home. But I was wrong.

Once back in Perth our communication came to a stop, I didn't hear from my dad at all for many years. The confusion of not knowing why my dad never ever spoke of me as his daughter to other people would have a massive negative effect on my life. I needed that sense of belonging that no one else could fill at this time.

I started to rebel…

At the age of fourteen it was a common thing for the kids in our year to attend parties and end up drunk but there was no way my mum would have let me go to these parties. I felt I was missing out. One Friday as me and my friends were walking home from school they were all raving on about this party. It sounded so cool and everyone was going except me. Hayley, who was my best friend, asked, "what's wrong Renee"? I replied, "there is no way mum would let me go", but then Hayley and I put our heads together and decided I would ask mum if I could stay at her house for the night. As soon as I got home I asked mum if I could stay at Hayley's and I couldn't believe it when mum said yes. I was so excited. This would be my first party.

When we got there I couldn't believe how old the guys seemed to be (and by old I mean thirty). But it didn't seem to bother anyone else, so I just accepted it. Then the UDL cans of bourbon started to come out. My friends were all drinking and smoking cones and I just tried to blend in, and before I knew it I had a can in my hand. Of course I was unsure but I didn't want to show that this was my first time drinking alcohol, so I just drank it, then I drank another and another.

It must have been close to midnight and everyone was so drunk and stoned, and someone said, "let's go for a walk". So off we all went. Even though we lived up in hills, there really was nowhere to go but we ended up at the local deli and before we knew it, we were breaking into the deli through the roof. One of my friends went through the roof first, then I was right behind her. I was so nervous and scared at the same time, and as I climbed through the hole I couldn't see anything on the floor or where to put my foot down, so I just took a chance and dropped down into the darkness, and man it was so cold. My friend was passing me things to pass outside for the others to put into a bag. I couldn't see a thing but I could feel everything was freezing – we had broken into the freezer. We climbed out and walked back to the party.

When everyone was unpacking the bag and pulling out sausage rolls and pies and cool drinks we were all laughing so hard. The next day I went back home trying to pretend everything was normal. Mum came in to talk to me and I pretended my grumpiness was just from lack of sleep, not a hangover. Although I didn't realise it at the time, this was where my addiction to risky behaviours started.

The next week back at school we were all talking about what we had done over the weekend, and the way it was glamorised made what we did all the more exciting and acceptable. From that weekend on the drinking became a regular occurrence and I realised more and more just how many people in our year were smoking pot and drinking alcohol.

Walking home from school one day me and Hayley called into Josh's house and we went down to the back shed. I used to often walk past his house and see all the kids from our year gathered in and around the shed, but I didn't know why. I soon found out. We went in and sat on the milk crates. Everyone was smoking cones through a can bong. Next it was my turn. I was so scared because of my epilepsy and my friends didn't know I had it. But that fear didn't hold me back, I still joined in. As we left, Hayley showed me a matchbox full of pot. She said, "how am I going to hide this from my mum", as her mum already suspected she smoked marijuana. I replied, "I'll take it for you and bring it to school in the morning", so I put the matchbox in my pocket. We got to the bush track that cut through to the back of our property, Hayley carried on to her place and I walked home.

When I arrived home my sister came to meet me asking, "why are you late?", "have you been smoking?" and I replied, "no, go away". Then before I knew it mum had heard our argument and came out to check for herself. My sister felt something in my pocket which confirmed to her what she was suspecting. Mum then asked to see it. I tried to pretend it was nothing but then things got out of hand, and me, Tammy and mum were all throwing punches and hits. But eventually they got the matchbox out of my pocket. Mum opened it up and asked, "what is this"? I told her it was tobacco but mum was not stupid as she used to roll her husband's cigarettes. She knew exactly what it was. Even though it wasn't mine there was no chance I was dobbing my friend in, so I just owned it.

CHAPTER TWO

# My First Criminal Charges

Mum was shattered but I didn't realise actually how much until I heard her call the police and tell them what I had inside the matchbox. The police arrived and took me back to the station and I was charged at Mundaring Police Station for possession of marijuana. I was to go in front of the Panel the following week.

The Panel is a place where first-time offenders have their charges heard in a place that is not as serious as a magistrate's court. If people learn their lesson and don't reoffend then they don't end up with a criminal record. It's like a chance before court.

When I returned home I went straight to my room. I was angry with mum for calling the police but at this stage I didn't even think about what my mum was going through. She came into my bedroom and said, "Renee, I don't know what to do with you now", as I was the only one out of all her kids who had started acting like this, messing around with drugs. She then told me we were going down to the Midland Department of Child Protection to see a case worker. Upon arrival I had no idea what to expect or what was going to happen next, but I soon found out. Between the case worker and my mum, they decided they would send me to a foster home in Cottesloe. So mum left. I really believe mum thought this move would scare me, then I would come home and be a good girl and change my behaviour. But it didn't.

When we arrived at the foster home the foster carers seemed really old, so I was unsure how we were going to get along, but they were really nice. They showed me around the house and showed me to my room. I had never seen such a massive bed in my whole life. When I sat on the bed my feet were left dangling. I was really tired as well as shamed, being in this new house with strangers, so I laid down and went to sleep.

First thing in the morning I wasn't even sure what to say to the carers so I told them I was going for a walk to the beach. That walk ended up with me being down the beach all day until it got dark, then I walked back to the house. When I walked in they told me how worried they were about me but I didn't know how to tell them that I just felt really uncomfortable in a strange person's house. They were lovely people, it was nothing they were doing wrong, but it wasn't home and I was just too pig-headed and stubborn to give in and call mum.

The next day my biological mum came down to the local deli, it was a few streets away from the foster home in Cottesloe. We sat down and she asked if I was OK, but deep down all I wanted her to say was, "OK, come on grab your things, you are coming with me". But instead she pulled out her purse and handed me $200, then she left. It left me feeling so confused, sad, alone, unwanted and angry. I couldn't understand how a mother would just leave her child in a foster home. It wasn't until years later that I found out the reason for this.

From that day on things went from bad to worse. I ran away from the foster home. The police got hold of me and took me to see my case worker in Midland DCP. I told him I didn't feel comfortable in a stranger's house with no other children. He found a vacancy for me to stay at a Snowy Bennet Youth Hostel in Midland...so off we went. When we walked in I was kind of scared as there were people everywhere. It looked as though I would be the youngest there; I could see teenagers up to young adults, some of them looked pretty scary, so it was time to put a hard front on.

One of the carers came up to me and led me into the office and did the initial assessment. Then they showed me through the hostel and introduced me to everyone. In the morning I met another girl, Angela. We went to Midland Gate Shopping Centre and hung out there, as we did a lot of our days. As time went by we met so many other kids in the same situation. Most of the kids weren't bad kids – they were just like me, lost, with absolutely no direction and looking for a sense of belonging. The longer we knew each other the more we seemed to look on each other as family.

One day everyone at the hostel was buying bottles of alcohol to go to a party that night. I put all the alcohol in my room because I thought I wouldn't get searched, being the youngest there. But I was wrong. We all got searched and I got caught out, so I was told to leave.

I went to the party that night with all my possessions in a backpack. I met a girl called Rebecca. We were drinking and talking out the front of the house and all of a sudden this car came sliding around the corner, then it was drifting up the street from one side of the road to the other. It pulled up at the front of the house and Rebecca seemed to know the guy who was driving. We got in the back seat and started talking, then we all heard sirens, the police were flying down the street with their lights flashing. The driver jumped out and ran and Rebecca jumped into the driver's seat. They gave chase all through

Midland. She lost them just before we pulled into Guildford Grammar School. Then all of a sudden there was a loud bang and the car came to a halt, we had hit a big cement pillar.

We jumped out of the car and ran towards the swampy area at the back of the school. By then the police had found the car so we were hiding in the reeds. We were so scared of the police finding us but also petrified by not knowing what was in the reeds; snakes, spiders, anything! But we had to lay low to avoid being seen by the police torches. It felt like we were there for so long before the police left. Once they did, we walked up to the train line trying our hardest to keep out of sight just in case the police were still in the area.

We made it to the train tracks. Still worried about the police we tried to lay low. While we were laying there trying to pass the time, Rebecca asked me, "where do you stop"? I told her about the incident with the hostel. Without any hesitation Rebecca said, "come and stay with me and my grandparents". So I did.

We arrived at Rebecca's just as the sun was coming up. We climbed through her bedroom window as quietly as possible trying not to wake her grandparents and her brother and his wife. Once inside, we lay on the bed and fell asleep. When we woke I wasn't sure how her family would react when they realised I was in their home, but I couldn't believe how welcome they made me feel and how accepting they all were. They never once made me feel like I didn't belong there. Immediately, I was part of their family.

Rebecca and I ended up walking down to the train station a few nights later and when we saw two of the same cars we looked at each other and both said, "come on", at the same time. She clicked one of the cars over and after I watched her I did the same to the other car. As we were driving through Guildford all of a sudden the car I was in just cut out. I was trying to click it back over but, nothing happened. I was so scared as I was parked in the middle of the road, and I definitely didn't look old enough to be driving, so I knew if someone had seen me they would have called the police. When Rebecca saw I wasn't behind her anymore, she turned around and picked me up.

Getting away with this made risky behaviours more and more exiting and addictive. After this we went through a period of stealing so many cars. We used to keep them for days and drive them around like they were our own. We found a vacant house with a big fence, where we used to park the cars in the backyard so they couldn't be seen, until one day the police came around to Rebecca's grandparents asking for both of us because we had been seen and reported by various people in the community.

We were taken down to the police station and charged or numerous car thefts and driving without a license. Rebecca's grandad came down and bailed us out. We were ashamed and embarrassed about getting caught, but that didn't stop our behaviour. We ended up having a big group of people who hung out together on a daily basis. We continued stealing cars, driving them all over Perth, doing fuel runs, or just driving them until they ran out of petrol then stealing another.

This risk taking behaviour continued and started us doing break and enters, wherever it looked like no one was home. I would walk up and knock on someone's door and if there was no answer we would jump the fence and get in wherever was easiest. Having got away with it so many times, it seemed like an easy way of paying for our alcohol/pot. At the time, in our heads, we didn't think we were hurting anyone. We didn't stop to think of what we were putting the home owners through. Now, I look back and I am so sorry to all the people whose privacy we violated; intruded into their homes, stole their belongings and went through their personal possessions.

This behaviour got worse and worse. We used to go up into the hills where homes were farther apart, so we were less likely to be seen and there were more places to hide. One day, between about five of us, we broke into every house on both sides of the road without being seen or heard. So the next day we went up to a different suburb in the hills and broke into another home. But at this home, while we were going through the bedroom we found a police uniform. We went to leave the house straight away but then we heard a car pull up in the driveway. We flew out the back door but the owner was coming down the side of the house, so we jumped the back fence and continued to keep cutting through backyards, jumping more fences to try to lose him. We had a car parked a few streets away. We finally reached it, jumped in and sped off.

We didn't return to Rebecca's until a couple of nights later. We snuck in through the window like always but in the morning we had a big surprise. The sergeant whose house we broke into was, unbeknown to us, actually Rebecca's uncle. He was one of the sergeants who had arrested me for possession of cannabis in Mundaring Police Station the year before. He had seen our faces as we were jumping fences…that's why he stopped chasing us.

This time we weren't so lucky getting bail. Due to our string of stolen cars and break and enters we were remanded in custody and sent to Longmore Juvenile Detention Centre. Now we were really worried, not sure of what to expect in this place at all, but we put our hard front on.

When we arrived they escorted us to the holding block. It was horrible. There was nothing but a cement block and brick walls in this little cell about the size of my mum's bathroom. We seemed to sit in there for hours before they came and did the initial assessment. Then it was time to take us into the shower block. We got undressed and were told to get into the shower to wash ourselves with a lice solution…man, it stunk so bad. Then they took us into the admissions block where they fitted us with their clothes and a pair of Dunlop Volleys. There was no style in this place. We were also given a kit bag which consisted of a change of clothes, bedding, comb, and a toothbrush and toothpaste – then the bag was used for laundry. We were escorted to our cells; I was taken to one cell and Rebecca was taken to the cell across from me.

Our cells were pretty bare, there was a bed, and behind a half cement wall was a stainless steel toilet and a shelf where we could stack our clothes. I made my bed and lay down to go to sleep.

In the morning unlock commenced at 6.45a.m. – time for showers. I wasn't sure what to expect. As we were being taken to the shower block I was thankful to see some familiar faces from town. We had breakfast, then we were taken to our classes for the day. At morning tea time, I noticed a girl I had had a fight with the week before at the Perth Train Station. As I was walking to get a drink this girl Mellissa came running up and jumped onto my back as if I was giving her a piggyback. She was punching me in the head but before I knew it the guards pulled her off. I think she was taken to the isolation block after that.

A few days later it was time to front court. The magistrate was really upset with our crime spree. He sent me to Warminda Bail Hostel and Rebecca was sent home with her grandparents under strict conditions.

I thought this was going to be very interesting because Mellissa had also fronted court that day and she had also been remanded to Warminda Bail Hostel. Mellissa and myself were put in a share room, but once we were up in the room by ourselves, Mellissa apologised for what happened at Longmore, and once we started talking she was alright, she just had so many problems and she was in such a bad place, emotionally, physically and mentally. I had never seen so many scars on arms so young, there seemed to be hundreds of laceration scars all the way up both her arms. We spoke quite a bit that day but then that night she had an argument with one of the workers and she just lost it. She smashed our bedroom window, punched into one of the workers, tried to run off, but I think she really just wanted to go back to Longmore where she felt safe. I never saw or heard of her again after that, but I quite often think about her wondering if she is alright.

By this stage I would have been about fifteen and a half, and my pattern of behaviour stayed the same, if not worse. I was in and out of Longmore more often than not. I became a very familiar face. If police tried to charge me with something, I would just plead guilty to the charge as it gave me a place to stay where I knew I had somewhere warm to sleep; there were showers and there was guaranteed food on the table.

The days I wasn't in Longmore, I would be hanging around drinking at a place called Tooweys Gardens in Midland, opposite the Junction Hotel. My family were at the point where if they needed to do any shopping in Midland they would try to avoid going to any of the places where they might run into me. If they needed to go to a particular place that was close to where I might be, then they would take a long way around in the hope they wouldn't see me or I wouldn't see them…life was definitely at one of my lowest points here.

This lifestyle continued until I was close to 17 when I put my pigheadedness, stubbornness, pride and shame aside and made contact with my mum. I rang her up and said, mum I need to change something here before something bad happens. I didn't feel I could do this much more. It didn't happen straight away but we started to meet for lunch once a week for about a month, then she said, "if you are willing to abide by the house rules, we can give it another go".

I went back home but it wasn't long before mum and myself had another argument. When we used to argue mum used to follow me around the house and keep yelling, no matter how much I tried to walk away from her, but not this time…she walked away and went to her room. I followed her to her room and sat on an exercise bike and started to ride it, tormenting her. Mum couldn't take any more. She came over and tried to pull me over the handlebars by my hair. I threw my arm up to break her clench and my forearm smashed mum straight in the nose. I heard the crack when it hit. What had I done? There was no way I meant to hurt mum. I said, I'm so sorry mum and ran away from home crying my eyes out. Once I built up the courage to ring mum a few days later, she told me I broke her nose. I explained to mum I was so sorry, and that I honestly never meant to hurt her. Thankfully, mum believed me. I didn't go back home…I was basically just staying wherever I could.

While I was gone this time, I started to get more and more violent. After drinking one day I went to Perth with a few friends and I ended up punching into this girl at the train station. I don't even remember why, but after punching into her she dropped her wallet, and I picked it up and me and my friends ran off. The police were chasing us all through the main streets of the city, we were ducking and weaving through the people and chaos of the city streets until we finally thought we had lost them. Feeling a sense of relief, we went into a gaming place called Timezone to try and to catch our breath. But sure enough a few minutes later the Police walked in, this time there was no where to run, so we sat in various gaming machines trying to blend in as if nothing had happened, but the Police knew exactly who we were.

I was taken down to the central police station. What I had done had been recorded on CCTV in Perth. I was charged with Assault Occasioning Bodily Harm and Stealing with Violence.

At this stage I knew if I didn't change my behaviour and attitude quickly, then I would surely be heading to jail for a long time.

CHAPTER THREE

# New Chance at Roadhouse Work

Mum spoke to my brother Brian's mother-in-law and father-in-law who owned Fortescue Roadhouse, and told them a bit about me and explained that I wanted to change my ways. Mum had asked John and Maria if they would give me a chance to work for them. I couldn't believe it when they said yes!!!

I went to mum's and packed some of my clothes, and mum took me to the bus depot. I was on my way to making a positive change in my life. I caught the coach up to Fortescue, and when I arrived Maria and John never once judged me for any of my doings. They never even once asked anything at all about it. It was straight out a fresh start. From this point on I was in control of handling my future.

I worked at Fortescue for eleven months, cooking, pumping petrol, serving customers. At cleaning time, we used to turn the radio up to max and we made fun out of mopping the floor dancing around the roadhouse. I think if people had seen us through the windows they would have thought we were mad. I stayed at the roadhouse, only going into Karratha once a month to do my shopping. Maria and I ended up getting really close. She taught me to smile and laugh again. We actually had so much fun working together; we would always be laughing and joking around. She made the best homemade pickles, and her braised steak and onions...it was the best!

One day Maria told me she needed to go to a wedding in Karratha and she was leaving Wendy, a lady in her mid-30s, and myself in charge of the roadhouse while they were gone. It didn't seem like too much to ask, as we used to get on OK. Wendy was a bit grumpy, but we hadn't had any problems in the past. The weekend came and Maria came in to say goodbye.

I still remember what she was wearing; she had a long green skirt on with a greenish floral pattern shirt. She looked so pretty as I had only ever seen her in her uniform dress and her apron. I said "have a lovely day" and off they went.

It was so hot that day, like 38 or 40 or something like that. I came in to give Wendy an order and she was so hot over the stove, I grabbed the water spray that me and Maria used to spray each other and ourselves with, and I sprayed Wendy. Well! She went troppo! She punched me in the face, so automatically I dropped a bomb on her, (which means punched her back) and she fell back and burnt her hand on the hotplate. The guy she was seeing at the time was the caretaker/yardman Gary. When he came in, and the way he was looking and talking to me, I felt like I had really stuffed up. How does something so simple, end up exploding into something so big. I was so ashamed about what happened. How was I going to tell Maria?

After my shift that day I went and packed all my belongings and booked a ticket for the coach that night. Then Maria and John arrived back, I explained to Maria what had happened. She then asked Wendy to leave. She tried to tell me I didn't need to go and she believed me, but I really felt like I let her down and I said, "thank you for everything, but I will still head off". Shame got the best of me here.

Once I was on the bus on my way back to Perth, our first stop was at Nanutarra Roadhouse. I went in to get a drink and the owner was behind the counter. He used to pull into Fortescue on his way to Karratha and we used to talk all the time. He asked why I was heading home and I told him what had happened. He suggested I go to Perth and have a couple of weeks off, then asked if I would come back up and work for him. I said I would.

On my return to Perth I caught up with some old friends. We went drinking and clubbing almost every night for the whole time I was home.

It was time for me to head up to Nanutarra. I arrived and the people there were good people, but I think that two weeks off gave me a taste for the drink again. I only lasted up there about four weeks then I was over it. I had been in contact with a girl called Christine while I was away, and she was telling me about a party that was on that weekend. That was it, I booked my ticket back home so I could make sure I was there for it.

This was another slip-up back into the same drinking pattern from before I went away. I started to get very aggressive once I started drinking. I was staying back at mum's, but I was out every night going to either footy, parties, clubbing, anything that involved alcohol and a big mob of people. After a few months mum was starting to get worried about me again, and I think I was starting to get a bit worried about myself as well.

My brother Peter and I hitchhiked up to Kalgoorlie hoping to get some work. We were staying at the backpackers. We were there for almost a week and money was getting very low. Mum had been talking to the lady on directory assistance (013) telling her Peter and

I were in Kalgoorlie looking for work, and the lady actually knew of a place where they had jobs going in a town called Leinster. We rang them up straight away and they gave us an interview over the phone. They asked if we had any bar experience. My brother Peter had plenty of experience, as he was in the Army and he did catering and bar work whilst there. As for me, I told them, "yes, I have had bar experience", but I just never told them which side of the bar that experience was. I knew that as I am a quick learner I could get the hang of things if I just watched what the other workers did. They told us to catch the bus up as we had the jobs.

I was shown to my room in the single men's quarters because my job was in the Sports Bar in Leinster. My brother was taken to Yakabindi, which was a mine just out from Leinster.

I learnt the ropes pretty quickly, except for pouring beer. That looked a lot easier than it was. I told one of the other bar attendants that the pub where I used to work only sold beer in cans, so then they helped me learn how to pour a beer.

I got on really well with all the patrons that came in. I had only been in the town about two weeks when I was talking to this guy who was a temporary bank manager. He was filling in for someone while they were away. It was pretty obvious he was trying to chat me up, I think I played on that a bit that day. I dropped a hint to him saying I needed to start saving up so I could buy a car. He told me to come down to the bank and see him the next day. I went into the bank after being in the town for two weeks with no ID, no references, and I left the bank with five thousand five hundred dollars.

Too lovely…

I had spotted a car that was for sale, and that was it! I bought it straight away knowing I didn't have a license, nor did I even think about the consequences of my actions. Now this was a really bad move on my behalf.

I worked hard and long hours while I was up there but my alcohol intake was very high, if not extreme. Some weeks my IOU was actually higher than my wage. One day while I was working, this man came in said, "hello Renee", I replied with, "do I know you?" He then went on to say, "I look different out of a blue uniform don't I". My heart just sunk, it was Constable Greg Norman from the Mundaring Police Station. He was one of the police who was in the station the day I was charged with possession of marijuana, and he had also arrested me for a few stolen cars when I was younger.

After seeing him I knew my time there was going to be short-lived as, if a person had a criminal record they were not able to reside or work in a closed mining town.

That night I went out to another single men's quarters just out of town. There was a band playing and the drinking continued all night, until almost morning. I was so drunk I have no idea how I made it back into town. I remember hitting one of the white posts on the side of the road and I tried to pretend it was on purpose, so I kept hitting as many as possible. When I arrived at the quarters where I stayed I started showing off doing figure 8s all over the grassed area outside the dongas. Then all of a sudden there were blue lights flashing and sirens blazing.

I pulled over. The policeman tried to do a breath test, and that's when the attitude came out. He asked me to blow in the bag and I refused. He asked again nicely, and I refused again. He then told me that I would have to accompany him to the police station. I was also reported for knocking down the white posts on the side of the road earlier. I tried to deny it but there was white paint all over my roo bar. I was then charged with Damage, No Drivers License, Reckless

Driving, Disorderly Conduct, Failing to Comply with a Preliminary Test, Excess 0.05.

After my appearance at court I was told to collect my belongings and leave town immediately.

When I was back in Perth I started to get into more and more trouble. I was drinking with friends in Midland, getting back into the same old routine. I ended up in two alcohol fuelled fights in the same day; I honestly don't even remember what they were about at all. Then a couple of days later the Midland Police saw me walking down the road and pulled on me. They took me down to the police station and charged me with Assault Occasioning Bodily Harm and Stealing with Violence…Now I really thought I was going inside.

I rang a friend of mine, Natasha, who lived out in Belmont. I explained the situation that I was in and asked her if I could come and stay with her and her cousin for a while, and she said yes. I moved into her house the next day.

CHAPTER FOUR

# Pregnant with Summer

I remember cooking bacon and eggs one morning and then that was it. I ran to the bathroom vomiting something terrible, I was feeling so sick. The next day, the same thing again...and the next day! I went to the doctor's and the doctor did a pregnancy test and it came back positive. What in the world am I going to do now? I was not ready for this!

I walked straight out of the doctor's surgery and straight into the bottle shop next door and bought a two-litre Jack Daniels. I started thinking, and the more I thought, the more I drank. I ended up drinking almost the whole bottle that day. I was trying to work out what I was going to do as I had so many charges still pending and I had 120 community hours outstanding. My behaviour was catching up with me.

The next day my head was killing me and my stomach was so sick it felt like I had some sort of poisoning. I decided 'no more', that was enough of the drink. I rang mum and asked her to come and meet me for lunch at Belmont Forum Shopping Centre. When she arrived we sat down and she knew exactly what I was going to tell her. We started to meet every week for lunch at the same spot. Mum accompanied me to all of my antenatal appointments; she was just as excited as me. This was the closest we had been since I was a little girl. My drinking was a thing of the past and I had quit smoking. I completed all of my community hours, but I couldn't stop stressing yet, as I still had to go to court on the assault charges. Mum helped me find a good lawyer and we applied for legal aid to assist with the fees. I was really worried this was going to land me in Bandyup as my record was so extensive, and the last thing I wanted to do was have a baby in prison.

It was court day, and I was seven months pregnant and there is nothing worse than having an unknown fate, not knowing if you are going to walk out the front doors or the back doors once the court case has been heard. But I couldn't blame anyone but myself for the situation I was in.

Standing there my knees were shaking. When the magistrate asked my name, I tried to say Renee Pitt without my voice trembling. Then he asked what is my plea? "Guilty," I replied. The magistrate started reading out the circumstances, I was so embarrassed and ashamed of what I had done.

Waiting for the magistrate to make his decision is torture, especially when they take their time. In the years before, none of this bothered me at all, but this time, because I felt I had meaning to my life, this outcome meant so much. The magistrate came back to give the sentence. He said, "I sentence you to 18 months imprisonment", and my heart just sank, but I couldn't say anything as it was MY behaviour that put me in this situation. But the magistrate continued saying, "suspended for 12 months". This meant if I reoffended in the following 12 months I would have to serve 18 months in prison.

I moved back into mum's house that same day and I just focused on being the healthiest that I could possibly be for my unborn baby. I wanted to ensure my baby was in the best possible environment when he/she was born.

Mum and I did everything together during this time. We went shopping for maternity clothes, organised my hospital bag, we rearranged the furniture and redecorated the bedroom at mum's to get it ready for the baby's arrival. We went looking for, and found, the perfect pram so we could still go walking up in the hills after baby was born.

I had two lists, each consisting of my five favourite names, five boys' names and five girls' names. Mum and I had a bet that if it was a boy then I would name the baby, but if it was a girl then she would pick a name off the list to name baby.

Mum was with me throughout the labour. She never left my side for a second. She walked with me up and down through the rose garden at King Edward Memorial Hospital. She held my hand every step of the way. Once baby was born I heard her yell, "it's a girl, I won", then mum cut the cord. When baby was rugged up we went back into our room. I asked mum, "what name have you decided on", and she replied, "do you think Summer Evelyn Pitt suits her", and I said "most definitely".

We went back home two days after Summer was born and she settled into her new home. When Summer was about six weeks old, mum and I were sitting in our bedroom watching TV. I was sitting on the floor with my legs crossed and I had Summer lying across my lap. I was about to go to bed and mum said, "could you just stay up and watch the end of the show with me"? I said, yes. After a few minutes I looked down and Summer's mouth was all blue, her hands were blue and her feet were blue. I shouted "mum" and threw Summer through the air to her. I jumped up and called the ambulance. Mum ran outside hoping the cold air would shock Summer and maybe help her start breathing again. The people on the 000 line said an ambulance should be here within a few minutes, and thankfully the ambulance was coming down Bunnings Road, which was at the top of our street. They were on their way back to Mundaring from Gidgegannup so they didn't take any time to get to our place. They revived Summer in the back of the ambulance. Once she was stable I jumped in with her and she was taken to Princess Margaret Hospital.

They did a whole heap of tests on Summer the following day to find out what was going on and they found she had blood in her urine. After more tests they found she had two urethra tubes, which meant the urine was coming down one tube and refluxing back up the other and diseasing the kidney. They organised for Summer to go into surgery ASAP.

Whilst they were in surgery removing the extra urethra tube they found that she also had two bladders, one inside the other, so they also removed one bladder and reconstructed a new bladder floor.

After this Summer recovered so well, she is definitely one strong survivor.

CHAPTER FIVE

# New Job Opportunities

A few months later mum and I were walking through Midland Gate Shopping Centre and I said to mum: "I might put my name down for some work." I put my name down at a few shops and the next day I got a phone call asking was I available to start the next day at Cut Price Deli. I went down and got along really well with the other workers and the boss Shirley. I worked there for about a year, then I applied to Centrelink asking them if they could help me fund a Certificate III in Secretarial and Administration at Olympia Business College. The funding came through – I was so excited.

I loved the course, it was a 20-week course and I completed the course with distinctions in every subject. Once this was finished they helped with job placement. I went for two interviews in the first day after completing my course, and believe it or not, I got the second interview that I went for, at Richard Ellis International Property Consultants in the city. I worked there as an assistant secretary. I got on really well with everyone there and I did well at my job.

About a year and a half later, I think I really just got bored and felt I needed to do something different, so I handed in my resignation and commenced working with Drake International and Kelly Services as a temp worker. I was working all over Perth; every week was at a different location.

One of my jobs at this time was at United Construction in Kwinana. I used to drive an hour and a half to work each way. I heard about a competition on the radio. I rang up and entered a 'Hands on a Hyundai' competition through 92.9*fm*. They selected ninety-two people who, at various locations across Perth, put one hand on a Hyundai, and the last person holding their hand on the car won it. Later that day I received a phone call to say I had been selected to be one of the ninety-two people. They placed ten people at eight cars at different locations, and twelve people at the other, all holding one hand on a Hyundai. Well, I was doing really well, we were going into the third day and there were people coming down and watching what was happening, and the contestants were either falling asleep or just making a simple error due to the tiredness. Then they were eliminated from the competition.

I had some old friends who came down and noticed me. I hadn't seen them for years. We were talking for ages, (well I wasn't going anywhere). We exchanged numbers and caught up on what had been going on.

At this stage there was only a man in Morley Hyundai left, and myself and another lady on the same car at Midland Hyundai. I think my mind just told me that enough is enough and all of a sudden at 4am in the morning, I just walked up to the urn and raised my hands to warm them up. I was out of the competition. The next day, that lady who was on the same car as me won.

I didn't win that car, but a couple of days later I went to a car yard in Midland and saw a gunmetal grey Holden Commodore VN SS. I fell in love with this car, even though it wasn't practical. I didn't even think about how much it would cost to run. I did have a good job, so

I thought I would be fine to make the repayments. Once I had the car, this was when I started to slip back into my old behaviour. I contacted my old friends. We would go drinking or clubbing every night after work. It didn't take long before my work standards started to slip, then I would miss days at work because I was still partying or still drinking from the night before.

After a few weeks of this I wasn't getting any more work from these agencies, and for good reason. So, of course, the money was getting less and less. I then worked out I could use my cheque book to pay for either petrol or drink, knowing the cheques would all bounce. I never thought about the repercussions of my actions at all.

One morning after returning home from the night before, mum told me the police had been around the previous day looking for me. I asked mum if she would watch Summer for me as I was going to take off and try to avoid jail for as long as I could. I didn't know it at the time but I was about to lose contact with mum and Summer for a while, and me leaving like this was making the gap between me and Summer so much bigger – the longer I was away the harder it was to make amends.

I went out with my friends that night and we were drinking up at Rocky Pool in Swan View and I told them I would be leaving the next day to go up north for a while. One of my friends then said "sure Booma". As soon as I got home I packed my things, said goodbye to Summer and mum, and off I went.

I left Perth with fifteen dollars cash and a packet of pizza shapes, but I bounced cheques for petrol the whole way to Karratha. As soon as I got there I went straight to K Mart where my sister had worked a few years before. She had put a good word in for me. I got a job from Monday to Friday from 7.45a.m. till 1p.m. then I went to CES to see what other jobs were available. I found another job – afternoon and night work at Hampton Harbour Boat and Sailing Club. This was in a place called Dampier which is a town just out of Karratha. I applied and got the job.

I went straight to the backpackers and told them I was new to town. I explained I had employment but I needed accommodation. I wasn't able to pay until the following week. They allowed me to fix my account up once I had been paid.

I was loving the night life up here; it was like a massive party every night. But as my drinking was getting way out of hand, it was hard to keep the funds flowing so I could pay for the drink. So, time to get a third job. I went and applied for a job at Nightclub 101 for Friday, Saturday and Sunday nights. While working there I ran into an old friend of mine from Swan View. She would come up to the bar and order roughly four drinks and pay with hundred dollar notes, then tell me to keep the change. Of course, this got my mind ticking…how could she afford to tip me so much? After work that night I met up with her and had a few drinks. Well, it wasn't long before a little bag of white powder was pulled out. With the glamour that came along with this little bag of white powder I was instantly attracted. At first I started to snort it, then as time went on it wasn't long before I was shown how to inject it. Once this commenced, what can I say, things went from bad to worse.

One night I had a Wild Turkey and Cola stubby as my "staff drink". I was driving home from work and the police pulled me over. They did a random breath test first and that stubby was enough to take me over the limit. While I was at the police station getting processed my other outstanding enquiries came up, so the police came back to where I was staying to search through my belongings to find any evidence in regards to the fraud allegations. When they were searching my belongings they found receipts and the cheque book I had been writing all the cheques from. I was charged with twenty-seven counts of fraud.

The next week I was to appear in front of Karratha Magistrates Court. I pleaded guilty to the excess 0.05 and I got the remainder of the charges remanded for legal advice.

The following day I was to start my shift in Dampier at 2p.m., so I just drove anyway, and sure enough on the way home I was pulled over and charged with driving under suspension. This happened every night after work for seven days. Then I knew I was in big trouble, but believe it or not I still drove to court the following week. While I was in the waiting room a man came in and asked me if my name was Renee Pitt. I replied, yes. He said, "could I please have the keys to your car"? My car had been repossessed.

That day I was remanded in custody for four weeks in Roebourne Regional Prison while they did a pre-sentence report. This is where a community correction worker comes and collects as much information about a person, their life circumstance and current situation. Then with this information it's easier for the magistrate to work out what sentencing is appropriate for the accused.

This could have been a very scary place if you didn't know anyone. It was co-ed, which means there were men and women walking around doing day-to-day jobs and/or activities together. Medium security prisoners mixed with minimum security prisoners – maximum security prisoners were held in a separate quadrangle but they could still have people sit and talk with them. I was thankful that when I walked in, I immediately noticed some people I knew from Perth.

On my next appearance in court I was released on a twelve-month Intensive Supervision Order. This meant I had to report on a weekly basis to a Community Corrections Officer. I was not able to leave the state, I had to do 120 community hours and I had to be good for the next twelve months because if I reoffended in that period I would have to do:-

- 12 months in prison
- Get re-charged for the offence that I received the ISO
- Plus the new charges
- Plus the sentencing for the new charges whatever they may be

So it was time to *try* to behave.

I came back to Perth to do my community service hours and I completed my ISO.

But I was missing the money from working so I went down to CES looking for some country work. I found they were looking for bar workers in Kalgoorlie. So up I went. I think I was working there for a few months before my behaviour went into another dive. My using became a daily occurrence. I met some of the locals and it was back into the self-destruct mode.

The majority of our days were a total blur, we were always that off our heads and living life so fast…fast cars, fast music, everything we did was flat out. We took whatever we could and as much as we could. The more "fried" we were the better. From "candy flipping", which is LSD and ecstasy at the same time, or individually along with the speed, it all depended on what we were able to get our hands on at the time. The moment we started coming down, or coming back to reality, it was time to get on again.

One day I borrowed a friend's car. It was a bombed up brand new Mitsubishi Mirage. I told them I was just going down to the shop, but I didn't say which shop. Not even thinking about what I was doing, nor about how much I was crossing the boundaries of our friendship, I ended up driving their car down to Perth, which was 700km away. As soon as I arrived in Perth, I went straight to pick up my friend Ricky and her uncle, Jason. Jason was already out on bail for about fourteen charges so we tried to not get up to too much mischief, or should I say, try not to get caught for what we were doing. We were driving around for a few days catching up with people and chasing whoever had the best gear at the time.

Later that night, and by later that night I mean it was about 4am, Jason was driving past Bandyup Women's Prison, and sure enough the first car we passed, was a police car. As soon as they saw us they dropped a U-turn.

We all went into panic mode, as we had gear in the car and none of us had licenses. Jason put his foot down as soon as he spotted them, he then pulled straight into the first side street and then into the first driveway and immediately we all jumped out, so the police didn't see who was driving the car. Jason ran and hid in the overgrown grass on the far side of the property.

Ricky was under a three-month suspension but she was working for a legal organisation in Perth so if she got any convictions she would lose her job. Jason had a few lifetime bans and was already out on bail for a whole heap of other charges and I had lost my license for seven years and I was only two weeks away from being able to get it back.

Ricky and I were standing next to the car and the police walked up to us and asked, "who was driving"? Neither of us said a thing. They asked again, "who was driving"? Again, neither of us said anything.

Before long another two police cars turned up, and they were getting closer and closer to where Jason was hiding. But once I saw the police dog arrive, and before they let the dogs out, I said, "it was me, I was driving".

At first they didn't believe me, but one of the officers then said, "why wait until now, before you tell us this"? I then went on to say, "this will now be my fifteenth time under suspension. I lost my license seven years ago, and I would have been able to get it back in two weeks. Wouldn't you keep quiet"? Immediately they stopped the search, thank goodness, as they were so close to finding Jason.

I ended up going to court and I pleaded not guilty because I knew I was going to get jail for this, so this brought me some time.

A friend of mine, Brooke, knew of some work going down in Busselton, which is a town about 300km south of Perth. So Hazel and I went down to give it a go. Hazel used to have a bad heroin habit before I met her, but since I had known her we only used speed. We would have been down there only about a week when one day I was walking through town and I saw Hazel talking to a guy in the park. I could see this guy was on the "smack" and I knew that her seeing this guy had given her the urge to get on the heroin. I was trying to act like the big sister and not let her go anywhere where she might have been able to get her hands on any. But when someone has that urge it is very hard to get through to them, sometimes it is impossible.

We ended up in a huge argument and that was it, she was out the door. I heard she went and met this same guy, scored off him, then went back to Perth.

I stayed down in Busselton and ended up getting a house through the lady I was working for. My life turned into a big party; if it wasn't the speed that was keeping me up for weeks on end then it was the ecstasy. We were going to raves every weekend, and every other night and day was a big blur. We organised to have a massive party at my house on New Year's 2000, a party I would soon miss.

It was only a few weeks after this that I found out Hazel had an overdose on heroin and died. She was so young. At the time of her death she was only 18 years old. She was such a funny chick. I will never forget the saying she used to always say if someone accused her of something: "It wasn't me, it was the one armed man and he ran that way."

CHAPTER SIX

# Back in Prison

I changed my plea to guilty, then had my court case moved to Busselton Magistrates Court.

The day of my court appearance I had been up for twelve days on ecstasy. As I was waiting for my name to be called, a friend of mine, Carol, rocked up. She said, "come into the toilets, I've got a going away present for you". We went halves in half a ball. A half a ball back then was about $600 worth. While she was mixing it up, I was thinking how much this was about to smash us both, but on the other hand, I was thinking well this will be my last taste for a long time. So we just had it.

We were "munted".

I was in the cubicle trying to wait for my eyesight to come back. I didn't even know if Carol was in the same state as me, I wasn't even able to talk, I was just way too smashed. Then there was a voice at the door, it was the Prosecuting Sergeant. He said, "Renee Pitt to the court room".

OK, well this was going to be interesting.

I was walking out of the toilet block and into the court room with my hand sliding along the wall, as my eyesight hadn't come back yet. All I could see was white. As I walked into the court my vision finally started to come back, I must have looked so messed up.

Standing there I knew the magistrate could see I was off my tree, and what a bad place I was in physically and mentally. I knew there was only one way out of the court room for me, and that was through the back door. The magistrate sentenced me to twelve months and one day with no parole.

Brooke and a few other of my friends who were there with me, were stunned. They couldn't believe I was not coming out. But when all of us were on drugs, there was no room for rational thoughts in any of our heads.

While I was in the holding cell at Busselton Police Station, I was that off my head I was going troppo. I do remember that I was in such a state that I was smashing my head into the cement wall while I was screaming some not so nice things at the police officers – I don't know what that was going to accomplish other than I was going to have a big headache once I came down off the drugs.

They then put me into the monkey truck (a police four-wheel drive with a cage on the back) so we could start the trip to Bandyup. We were about to drive out the driveway and Brooke and the others who were at the court with us, tried to block the driveway to stop the car from leaving the station.

Looking back, I have no idea how they actually thought they could do anything to stop the police. And it just goes to show that when you are under the influence of drugs, some crazy thoughts go through your head, and these thoughts are just and make sense to that person, no matter how irrational they seem to someone else not on drugs.

Police came from everywhere that day, and in full force as they don't mess around. Everyone who was involved with trying to block the police vehicle ended up getting smashed by the officers and they were charged with hindering police.

Even though I didn't realise it at the time, I believe at this point in my life prison was the best thing that could have happened, because the way that I was living life, well, I wouldn't be here today writing this story if I didn't have something pull me up…like a year in prison.

I needed to pull up or have something pull me up, as I was in self-destruct mode.

Once I got up to Bandyup I slept for the first few weeks. My body was trying to catch up and recover from what I had been putting it through. I was OK in there as I knew so many people. But being in prison you need to keep yourself busy to pass the time. If you sit around not occupying yourself, your days can go so slow and you end up doing you time really hard. I was working in the laundry, washing, drying and folding and sorting clothes. When you first arrive in prison, your security rating starts at maximum then after a few weeks the officers do an assessment to bring your rating down to medium, then a couple weeks after that you go down to minimum. Once you are at minimum security you can be transferred to a minimum security prison.

After a couple of months my security rating went down and I was transferred to Nyandi Women's Prison in Bentley.

While I was in Nyandi, one of the officers came into my cell and said: "Pitty, you're wanted up in the office." I was told I had a special phone call from one of my sisters. I could hear the seriousness in her voice. She went on to say, "Renee, I've just come home from a counselling session and lots has come up from the past. I need to tell you something". I said, "what is it"? She said, "it's about what happened between your biological mother and Darren", who was my dad. I always knew there was something I wasn't told about. Now I am finally about to find out. She then said, "it wasn't consensual Renee. I was sitting outside the door and I heard everything. He forced her and I was so young I couldn't do anything to stop it". She continued, "it didn't just happen once Renee, it happened so many times".

I know how badly this messed my sister up having hidden it for so many years, as she was talking about the way I was conceived and my age now is twenty-one. She had hidden this secret all my life.

I hung the phone up after talking to her and I had no idea how I was going to take any of this in. This is a serious issue for any person to take in. All I remember thinking was "what the…how does someone do this and get away with it", and "why would someone do this to another human being"?

Having heard this, it did kind of mess me up in one way, as no one wants to hear a story like this about themselves, but then, it answered so many questions I had in my head. From hearing this I was able to work out that every time my biological mother would see me, she would remember what happened to her, and every time my dad saw me he remembered what he had done.

This also answered another question I had in my head.

This question was how my biological parents could leave me and not step in when they knew I was in a bad mental state, on drugs, on the streets and in dangerous situations and environments. My initial belief after finding out this information was that my biological parents must have been hoping I would get rid of myself through my lifestyle – whether it be through an accident or through overdose. If

I wasn't around anymore then they wouldn't have the past haunting them.

If this is true or not I suppose I will never know, but this is how I felt inside.

While I was in Nyandi, I started off working in the kitchen with Natalie, Julie, Amanda and a few other girls. We used to always try to have fun as it made the days go faster. But I think we must have got on the officers' nerves some days acting like hyperactive children. One day I was messing around with the girls as always and the head chef, Patrick, came in yelling, "that's enough Pitty, you need to settle down". My response was a bit over the top but as I have said before I was a bit poxy (cheeky) at this time in my life. I shouted, "f…. you Fatprick". He kicked me out straight away.

It was a few months into my sentence and I was able to apply for home detention. It was approved to commence at mum's house in Chidlow. The second I was released, I immediately tried to bend the rules. Mum's house was across the road from the local football oval and it wasn't long before I worked out I was able to go over there without the alarm going off. Another part of the home detention was the Community Corrections Officers who have an automated calling system where a machine would call the house phone and once this call was connected I needed to place my electronic wristband into a device that was joined to our phone. By doing this action it would confirm I was where I was meant to be. After a couple of days, I worked out that if I missed one call, they would call back a few minutes later. Knowing this, I worked out I could go over to the oval, and if I missed a call, then mum would be able to call my mobile and let me know…that would give me just enough time to run home before their second call.

My drug use soared here, as I got one of my friends from Midland to come up and drop enough drugs at home to last me a few days.

I remember we looped so hard one night, me and a few of my friends actually pulled up a massive patch of lawn in mum's backyard. When I say massive, I mean like the size of an above-ground pool, and when she woke up and saw what we had done, well, she went off. We told her we were planting a garden for her. This was something that was never to be completed.

Deep down I knew I couldn't do the home detention and be successful with it. Continuing with it, especially when I wasn't willing to try to do it the right way, wouldn't be fair to mum. I had to sleep in the lounge room so that I was right next to the phone. Then, every night the security officers would come around and knock on the door to check I was home – and besides, my behaviours were fully intruding on my mum's and my daughter Summer's life.

It was in my second week on home detention when I rang up Miss Malone, the superintendent in Nyandi, and asked her: "Miss, how can I come back to jail?" She then told me what she had to do and told me to pack my stuff and wait for the Mundaring Police to come and collect me. She then organised the return-to-prison order for me.

Once back in Nyandi, I felt so much better. It was just not fair on my mum to be putting her through all the stress of my anger outbursts and my loopy behaviour.

Mum used to come and bring Summer down to visit every weekend. I used to look forward to seeing them both every week and spending time with Summer doing activities with her or just playing a game with her.

But due to me not being around much, Summer found it hard to get close to me, as the only time she had seen me on a regular basis was when I was in prison.

I put my name down for the work camp in Toodyay. We were doing things like cleaning graffiti off walls and cleaning up all along the sides of the river and picnic areas. It was hard work but it made the time go by so much quicker than being back at the prison. We used to go up to Toodyay on the Monday morning and stay there till Friday, then come back to the prison for the weekend and collect our shopping, like smokes or tobacco, toiletries, snacks and cool drinks. It was good as it kind of broke the weeks up.

I remember one weekend I arrived back and I had run out of smokes the day before. I went to go collect my canteen order and it hadn't been put through. I was furious. There is nothing worse than being in jail and not receiving your spends that you look forward to, especially when it is cigarettes.

I was going troppo as it's not as if I could go down to the local deli and buy some more. I rang Brooke and asked her if she could throw me some over the fence. I wasn't even thinking about the fact that sneaking anything inside a prison is classed as "trafficking", it doesn't matter what it is. Brooke came straight down and threw them over exactly where she said she would. Oh, that cigarette was bliss when I finally had it.

Later that night one of the officers Miss Brown came in to our room and said, "hey Pitty, come with me". I knew exactly what this was about. She went on to say: "Pitty, look you're in deep shit. I've been listening to the telephone recordings as always, and I heard your conversation about the cigarettes. You're going to have to come down and see Miss Malone the superintendent." She went on to say, "you know you could be sent back to Bandyup for this till the end of your sentence"?

I fronted Miss Malone and told her I knew I did something I wasn't meant to, but I had been away all week up at work camp and somehow, my order never went through. All I wanted was a smoke.

Miss Malone told me, "by rights Renee, you should be out of here for that, but you'll want to be on your best behaviour from now on". Thankfully, I got along well with everyone there and I think they had a soft spot for me, as even though I was in jail, I always tried to have fun and put a smile on the girls' faces.

Jail can be a very dark and lonely place to be in.

Jail can also be a very dangerous place to be in.

Days in jail can go so slow when you're doing it hard.

That's why I made it go the fastest way possible; I kept that smile on my face always, as a smile is very contagious. One thing that used to bring me through my hardest times was me putting that smile on my face, then automatically someone would smile back.

Once I got out after that year things were still going pretty bad because while I was inside I lost my house, my furniture, my clothes and my possessions. I had no idea how I would start over from scratch. My speed habit just got so bad it was the first thing I did each day, and the moment I started to come down I was off to get it again.

CHAPTER SEVEN

# Meeting Jer

It was my 23rd birthday, January 7, 2001, and I was hitting a real low point. I felt like I had two options; go back inside where I had a routine and some stability, or do something to myself. I just didn't seem to have the fight to start going through this all over again.

Then I got a phone call from Brooke. She could hear how down I was. She said, "where are you, I'm coming to pick you up". Once she arrived I started to feel a bit better. She said we were just going to call into one of her friend's places, his name was Jerremy.

When we pulled up there would have been about 20 guys out the front of this Mirrabooka house. Brooke went inside and I waited in the car. She used Jerremy's phone to call me from inside to make sure I was OK, and unbeknown to me Jerremy saved my number.

A couple of months later I was working at a roadhouse south of Perth and one night I got a text message saying, "smile, you just got a message from a fucking legend"! Immediately, I rang the number and said, "who's this", and the voice on the other end said, "you don't know me but I'm Brooke's friend Jerremy". We sat on the phone and talked all night and eventually fell asleep while we were still on the phone. The next day, the second I finished my shift, we were on the phone again until we fell asleep. This happened every day for the next two months until I came back to Perth where I shared a house with my sister Olivia. I knew I had fallen in love with him since that very first phone call. My first night back we arranged that he would be come over for dinner. I couldn't wait to meet him.

I was so nervous, and excited, all at the same time…I couldn't even explain the feeling, but all I did know was that this was the happiest I had ever felt in my whole life. I knew I had finally met my match. I made apricot chicken and rice, then waited for him to arrive.

When I saw him walking down the driveway in his blue jeans, bright yellow FUBU jumper and bright yellow FUBU cap, I remember thinking, "too lovely". He just oozed style.

After that we didn't spend much time away from each other at all. If he wasn't with me at Olivia's then he was driving around with his brothers Dwayne and Mat, but that whole time, I would be sitting on the BBQ at the back of Olivia's on the phone to him for hours and hours at a time. He had one phone for me to call him on and another phone for everyone else to call him on.

One night while I was on the phone to him I could hear police sirens in the background, but then they would fade, then a few minutes later I would hear them again and then they would fade. I asked him what are you doing, he replied, "about three hundred down the Freeway", in a stolen WRX. They were slowing down and waiting for the police to catch up, then they would take off again. Hearing this only made me want him more, as he too had the same love for risky behaviours.

It wasn't long before I fell pregnant and then the sickness set straight in.

We both had an addiction to meth, an addiction that together we were not able to conquer.

Eventually, due to my lifestyle choices, my sister and I had an argument and I moved out of her place, and moved into a house in Princess Road, Balga. Well, it wasn't long before this turned into an open house.

Life in this house was so full on, but yet it appealed to me. Every day was full of crime, drugs, money, car chases, stolen goods, dodging police and violence.

This was the only life that we both knew, and when you have addictions you just do whatever you have to do to support that habit.

CHAPTER EIGHT

# Arrival of Children

One weekend we went out to June's (Jerremy's mum) to see his daughter Sasha and to have a BBQ lunch. Sasha was aged seven but she had lived with her nanna since she was a toddler. She used to call me "cool bananas" as this was a saying I used to use often. While we were there June said, "oh, the other kids will be here in an hour". I responded with "what kids"? She went on to say, "Jerremy's kids, they are coming down to stay for a year". "Oh wicked," I said, "and where will they be staying?" She then continued to tell me, "with you and Jerremy". Well, did my head spin like you would not believe. I didn't even know how to talk to a kid let alone look after one. I was soon about to learn.

We went to the bus depot and I was introduced to Abbey 14, Dakota 12, Isaiah 3, and Trinity 2. Abbey and Dakota went to June's house to stay and Trinity and Isaiah stayed with us. There was only one of his kids who didn't come down, James, he stayed up in Kununurra.

Once we arrived back at the Princess Road house, Jerremy was out at the car talking with a few boys in the driveway, so Trinity, Isaiah and myself were sitting in the lounge room, and I was trying to think of a way I could break the ice. Then all of a sudden I stood up and started singing Jeramiah was a bullfrog and they joined in. We became really close after that day. They were such good kids.

Once the kids moved in with us it was time to get out of the house in Balga. Jerremy's aunty had a caravan out at Jacaranda Caravan Park in Wanneroo and she let us take over her lease so the kids could be in a better environment. Then eventually, when a bigger caravan was available at Ocean Reef Caravan Park, we moved there.

Katie, the kids' mum, and I stayed in touch so I could keep the communication open with her on how the kids were going. She rang me one day to let me know she was coming down for a while to sort out some family issues. Katie had asked if she could come and stay with us for a few weeks as she didn't have any other family members down here. At first I was a bit unsure as this was Jerremy's ex of nine years, but I thought, "don't be stupid Renee, this would be a good chance for the kids to see their mum".

A few nights after Katie arrived, it would have been about 1a.m. Jer came home after being out doing 'bisso'. He had been awake for close to two weeks. He could see I was having a bit of pain in my stomach but I still had about a month to go, so I didn't think it was labour. Before he fell asleep he asked me again, "are you sure you're right"? I told him I was fine. As the night went on the pains got more intense and more frequent. OK, I was in labour, but how was I going to wake Jer up and tell him? By this stage it was 2.10a.m. and Katie said, "Renee you're going to have to wake Jer cos your contractions are getting close now", so I did. Jer called a taxi and it arrived at 2.20a.m. – we seriously thought that baby would be born in this taxi. My contractions were so close, and the taxi driver drove so fast to get us to King Edward Memorial Hospital in Subiaco. We arrived at the hospital at 2.55a.m. and they rushed us straight into the delivery suite and on the $10^{th}$ of June 2002, at 3.30a.m. a baby boy was born weighing 5 pound and 14 ounces. Jer sat on the recliner right next to his newborn son and said, "his name is Tyrone Mat Kennedy", then we both fell asleep.


Within a week of Tyrone's birth we applied for, and got, a house in Wanneroo. Finally, out of the caravan park! We also found a house for Katie and the kids to rent just around the corner from our house. It was good because the kids were still close to us.


When Tyrone was eight weeks old, Jerremy's mum, June, went into hospital and had a major asthma attack. This asthma attack was so severe she was put into an induced coma.

Once we heard what had happened we headed directly over to Joondalup Health Campus to see her. They told us she was in the Critical Care Unit. I gave Tyrone to one of his family members to hold as he couldn't come in to that area of the hospital. Seeing their mum this way, with all the tubes and hooked up to so many machines, absolutely broke the whole family. June was the entire family's rock. There is no other way to describe her role in the family. After the hospital that day Jerremy sat on the front passenger floor of his VL Commodore and just broke down.


Jerremy seemed to go into a depression after this as he didn't know how to deal with seeing his mum this way.

Some days it was so hard to get him out of bed to go over to see his mum but I felt I had to try to get him there.

If I woke him up and he wasn't in the right state to be able to see his mum, he would literally chase me out of the house with a cricket bat or he would jump in his VL and try to run me over. At times like this I quickly learnt which gardens I could jump into, as some gardens had brick edging or cement walls etc, where his car couldn't get to me. Then he would be worried about the owners calling the police, so he would just keep driving to someone's house until he cooled down. Days like this I would just go over to see June myself, and even though she couldn't answer me back, I really felt like she heard me when I would tell her that she really had to wake up and get better as her sons were going off and not coping.

At this stage in our lives the violence went from really bad to seriously extreme.

A few months later Jer's family came over for a visit and Jerremy's uncle said, proud as punch: "Jer, my missus is pregnant with baby number ten." Jer's response to this was, "hey unc, my missus is pregnant with twins". At this time Tyrone was only about three months old. I looked at him and said, "your cheeks".

Sure enough, after that little comment I started to get sick and yes, I was pregnant. When I went for a dating ultrasound I couldn't believe what I saw. At first there was one baby in a sac, and then another nurse came in and she said, oh, look there's another. My immediate response was, "what, where"? After she pointed to the screen I could see the second baby in its little sac. She then went on to say, "is that another"? Yes, there was another sac but it was empty. I then asked that lady if she could please leave the room as I didn't want her to see anything else. Jer was right as always, I was pregnant with twins. When I left the ultrasound place that day I rang Jer's mum, and told her it was twins. But I think she knew anyway. She was so excited, and I was so scared. I then rang Jer and said, "I hate you". I didn't really, I just couldn't believe he was right. He then said, "twins, unna"? I said, "yes", he was shouting with joy "BOSS"!

At this stage in our relationship – with the depression that set in with Jer, my pregnancy hormones being out of whack, along with the drugs and the extreme emotions that fly from them – our domestic violence went through the roof.

I remember after an argument one day when things had cooled down, I said to Jer, "I can't do this much more, every second day getting punched into". He said, "not every second day". I then said to him, "well Jer, out of 400 days how many of these day would you say you punch into me". He replied, "about 200". We then looked at each other with a kind of smirk.

Nineteen times in six months the police were called to our house, not by me but by the neighbours hearing our disputes. The neighbours must have been so sick of us. They didn't call the police every time, they would only call them if things were so out of control and they thought something bad was going to happen to me.

Looking back and walking through these years, I have no idea how I am still here.

One day after we had both been shouting abuse from different rooms he came into the kitchen, and things got out of hand rapidly. He punched me straight in the mouth. This hit lifted me that much my feet left the ground, and when I landed I split my elbow open on the kitchen bench. He then punched me again and again, but this time I dropped a king hit on Jer and he had an open mouth. I couldn't believe what I had done. I was so scared, I ducked and ran under his arm, then took off out the front door. I ran and kept on running.

I didn't return home until later that night, I snuck up to the window, hoping he wasn't right there waiting for me. Once I heard his snoring I snuck into the house and quietly laid in the bed. He then put his arm over me and said, "I thought you broke my jaw you pox", but then we both laughed.

It didn't seem to matter how extreme our arguments were, every night when we laid next to each other all the arguing was gone and everything was OK. We knew we loved each other, but we just had no idea how to communicate with each other.

We would find out how to get through our communication barrier a few years from now.

Tyrone at this stage had only just turned nine months.


When I was six months pregnant I went for a scan to see how things were going. Everything looked fine, babies looked healthy and they were laying crossways head to toe. The next day I started to get cramps in my stomach. Again I didn't think I was in labour as I still had three months to go. But the cramps got worse and worse. Then I found I was bleeding. I told Jer, he said, "get in the car". It was 4p.m. on a Saturday afternoon. We lived in Wanneroo near the high school and we made it to King Edward Memorial Hospital in twelve minutes, and that included us stopping at a friend's house, Sue in Hamersley, to drop Tyrone off, and driving past our friend Kate to say, "come to the hospital". We had driven past police at Stirling Gate Shops and were hoping for an escort but they didn't even see us. This trip that took us 12 minutes usually takes 35 minutes if you get a good run.

Once in the hospital the nurse at first didn't think I was in labour because I was so early in the pregnancy. I remember her saying, "it's highly unlikely that you're in labour already", then a contraction started to come. I yelled at her, "see I told you". She then said, "I'll wait for this contraction to finish then I'll examine you". Once it had passed she lifted the sheet then said, "I can see a limb, we have to stop this now". Everything from that point on was a mad panic. The doctors told Jerremy that we were lucky he drove so fast, as Paige was coming out sideways and if my waters broke I would have automatically pushed and that would have snapped her neck. They gave me a needle in my stomach to stop the labour and then rushed us through for an emergency c-section. There were doctors everywhere, at one point Jerremy counted 21 doctors and nurses in the one room. They had a sheet up so we couldn't see what was going on.

This was one of the scariest days of my life. Not knowing what was going on with our babies.

It was the 15th of March, 2003, and twin girls were born. I asked Jer to go make sure they were OK, so while my anesthetic wore off, he went down to the Special Care Nursery to check on them. He gave them a kiss and off he went.

I remember waiting for him to come back to let me know how they were going but as the anesthetic wore off and I was taken back to the room, Jer still wasn't anywhere in sight. I finally asked for the hospital phone to call him. I was furious, I thought he would have let me know how the girls were. Once he answered I shouted, "where the f…. are you"? "What's wrong," he said, "I'm just at Sue's picking up Tyrone." I said, "you could have just come and told me the babies were OK".

"Sorry," he said – he didn't even think about that, he was just so excited that he had to tell Sue and her partner that we just had two baby girls.

Due to the twins being born twelve weeks early, Jayde was very anemic and she had to have a blood transfusion when she was two days old. She also kept forgetting to breathe so she was kept under close watch until she was more stable. Paige was fine, she just slept all the time.

They ended up staying in the hospital for six weeks before coming home. When they did come out of the hospital they came home head to toe in a baby capsule they were that small – they were still size 000000 at six weeks old.

Once the girls came out of hospital I was given a case worker from the Best Beginnings Department because I had a multiple birth. They basically just help out any parents who have multiple births for the first year.

CHAPTER NINE

# First Attempt at Trying to Get Off

I was trying to cut down my using to attempt to get off. But when everything you do and everyone you know revolve around drugs it is so hard to keep yourself in the same surroundings and just quit.

I tried to organise with an aunty of mine, if I could come up to her farm to try to get myself clean, but a few days before I was due to head up there mum rang to tell me my aunty actually had a nervous breakdown.

I was crying on the phone to mum saying, "how will I ever get off the drugs"? After this phone call I was lying on the bed crying and I received a call from Julia, my case worker. I tried to stop crying so she couldn't hear how upset I was, then I answered the call to hear her happy voice saying, "hi Renee, I was just going to call in and drop you off some milk", I replied, bursting out, "yes please, cos I want to have a talk with you".

When Julia arrived, I invited her in and before I disclosed any of my thoughts to her, I said to her, "Julia, before I tell you anything, you can see my kids are all love, and all cared for, they have a clean house, they are not going without anything". She replied, "yes Renee, why?" I then went on to say, "I have a drug addiction, that I have no idea how to get off". She was stunned. She went on to ask me what I was addicted to and when I told her methamphetamine, she said, "I wondered how you did it".

From this day on Julia worked with me more and more. Over time she soon found out about the domestic violence, so she helped me get the kids into full-time daycare, to try to ease the stress in the household.

Three babies in a nine-month period would be stressful enough to the average family that didn't have any addiction problems. But with depression, drugs and the violent outbursts associated with them, added to the people coming and going through our house, the stress at times was unbearable.

I had meetings with Julia and her manager on a regular basis. Due to my being honest with them they worked with me to go on the waitlist to get into a residential rehabilitation facility where I was able to take the children.

I finally had a date to attend the rehab.

I packed the kids and my stuff ready to go.

My only concern was with the rehabilitation program being only twelve weeks, and I was worried about disrupting the kids from their daycare routine. I wanted to keep them in their normal lives as much as possible, and Julia and her manager thought that would be a good idea. They had actually organised a driver to pick the kids up from the rehab centre and take them to daycare in the mornings and bring them back in the afternoon.

I thought everything was going to be OK.

But the day before I was due to go, I got a phone call from Julia's manager to tell me the CEO at the rehab centre didn't like the plans we had made and said it would disrupt the program.

My heart sunk. With this letdown I stopped trying and convinced myself this change was never going to happen.

The support from Best Beginnings came to an end when the twins turned two years old, and I was too scared of the Department of Child Protection to have anything to do with them for the fear and reputation of them taking children away from their families.

When the twins were two years old Jayde was rushed to hospital with an allergic reaction to conjunctivitis ointment. We borrowed Jerremy's aunt's car to visit her at Joondalup Health Campus. On our way home from the hospital we were driving through Wanneroo and a police car pulled in behind us and put their sirens and lights on. As Jer didn't have a license and he was already due to go to court the next week, he floored it and the police gave chase.

If you had seen the car we were in you would have been just as surprised as me. It was a 1989 Ford EB. The gearbox was that bad, even at a slow speed it took off slow, then you had to wait for it to clunk into gear (that's the only way I know how to describe it).

Jer took the wrong side of Wanneroo Road to shake the police. He was driving in the middle of both lanes and all the oncoming traffic were pulling up on the verge so we didn't hit them. This gave us enough of a break that we got away. We went to a friend's close by and pulled the car into our friend's backyard, behind the gates so that the police wouldn't spot it.

We waited here for a few hours, then tried to take the car back to Jer's mum's. We were almost there. We were turning off Hester Ave onto Baltimore Parade, and you wouldn't dream of it, but that same

RTA police car was coming down the other side of the road and spotted us.

That was the start of another chase right through Clarkson.

Jer tried to cut through a park and when we hit a copper log, the roo bar snapped and went straight through the radiator and the car was going about 3 or 4km per hour. I said, "where are you gonna go now Jer"? His reply was immediate: "I'm going to my mum's." Driving up to June's there were so many police cars behind us; undercover cars, RTA cars, monkey trucks (which are a police 4x4 with a cage on the back), motorbikes and a helicopter. There was no way in the world we would get away this time. As we were driving up Baltimore the police were trying to go around us to block us off, but Jer just cruised along at the slowest speed going, swerving the vehicle from side to side so they couldn't get in front of us. We could hear the police on the loudspeaker saying, "this is the police, please pull over", but Jer just kept calmly cruising along.

We pulled up in his mum's driveway and police came rushing from everywhere. Jer knew exactly what he was doing as his mum came rushing out and stood straight in between Jerremy and all the officers. June shouted, "what's going on"? Then Jer jumped out, being cheeky, shouting out, "yeh, what's going on"? This was his sarcastic side showing. He was charged with sixteen driving charges from this one chase.

There are so many stories and adventures in every chapter of our lives. If you knew Jer you would know what I mean, he was one of a kind. He could make the sourest person laugh their heart out, sometimes just by taking the piss out of them.

CHAPTER TEN

# Funniest Day Ever – Jers Sarcasm

One day Jer had a really bad ear infection, and my sister Olivia and I took him to the doctors in Wanneroo. The doctor was a bit rough when he went to examine his ear and you could see the pain in his face. All he said was, "Renee, tell this c…t"! I did, and the doctor said, "you are going to have to go to Sir Charlie Gardener Hospital".

To take Jer's mind off the pain of his ear he was tormenting me all day, so much so that all that I could say to him was "get f….cked you black c…t". His response to me that day was priceless. He said, "now that's enough of the racist stuff Renee…just think of it this way, we are all green except, I'm dark green and you're light green". This is the kind of sarcasm he was full of.

We headed down towards Nedlands, but before we got there we had to get him registered with Medicare. Once we got to the front of the line and the lady called "next please", we got to the counter and the lady asked for his name, and then she asked his nationality. He looked at me shocked and said, "she thinks I'm a boat person, well that wouldn't be a very smart people smuggler would it. What, the only people that could fit on the boat would be me and the person driving it". I lost it laughing. We were then asked to fill in a form and then return to the line.

While I filled in the form for Jer, he went to get us a drink each. I waited in the line for him to get back and when he did he took a big mouthful out of his Fanta. I don't know what went through his mind, but he burst out laughing and sprayed this lady in front of him with a massive mouthful of cool drink. If only you could have seen this lady's face, it was totally and utterly repulsed and disgusted. This lady looked like she was from Peppermint Grove or Dalkeith, which are Perth's richest suburbs, and he had showered her with Fanta out of his mouth. It was hilarious, but this lady definitely didn't think so.

We finally got all his paperwork completed then continued to the hospital. Well, usually it takes hours and hours to get seen by a doctor there, but while we were sitting in the waiting room, Jer was still tormenting me and I was going troppo. Then a nurse came up and said, "excuse me sir, but if you are going to use obscene language then we will have to ask you to leave". He then replied to her in his nicest possible but sarcastic voice: "I am most terribly sorry ma'am but I don't believe I swore at all." And that was it; they pushed us through to see the doctor and we were out of there within twenty minutes.

On the ride back home he was still tormenting me, and my sister was finding it so hard to hold her laugh in. I couldn't take it anymore; I jumped out of the car that quickly at the Leach Highway lights and yelled, "you two can go along, I'll walk home". I had forgotten to grab my shoes off the floor of the car and when I was walking across the grass I walked into a big patch of double gees, which are prickles with very large spikes. I was pretending the frustration wasn't getting to me but I couldn't hold it. I jumped up and down stomping my feet. Then after a while I realised I needed my shoes to walk anywhere, so I bit my pride and got back in the car. Finally, he promised he wouldn't torment me anymore.

We went through so many ups and downs over the years. But we weren't going to let anything get between us; we just stayed together and got through whatever situation we were in at the time. Our lives were so explosive in every which way, but we knew we loved each other and wanted nothing more than to be together.

The violence in our relationship was fuelled by the meth and the lifestyle that came along with that, along with the fact that we didn't know how to communicate and express our feelings to each other. Jer grew up in Balga, and it's not the normal thing for these boys to be sensitive and romantic, or even to express their emotions, it's just not heard of.

And as for me, I believed if someone expressed their feelings then that would be seen as a kind of weakness, so it just didn't happen.

So, if something was bothering us, neither of us knew how to express it so we would bottle it up until that feeling would just come out through an explosion. Once one person explodes then, of course, the automatic reaction for the other person is to explode back.

This explosive behaviour continued until 2005 when I got pulled over for driving under suspension. When they searched me they found I had a bag of meth. Once I attended court I applied for the matter to be sent to the Drug Court, as I knew this was my only hope to stay out of jail.

Drug Court is a court imposed order where you have to do three urine samples a week and attend a weekly court appearance to let the magistrate know how you are going, and then they tell you the results of your urine tests. Everything runs on a points system from one to ten. On commencement of the program you start at five and if you have a dirty test – a dirty is when a urine sample comes back positive to a drug, in my case methamphetamine – then you add a point, and if you have a clean test then you take off a point. You cannot exceed ten. If you do then you have to go into prison for five days to bring the points down, but if it happens too many times then they can breach you and you remain in prison until either a rehab is organised or, if you don't want to do rehab, then you just complete your sentence inside.

While I was on assessment for Drug Court, which is the first four weeks of Drug Court, out of forty-six piss tests I had forty-three dirties, as I was trying to find a way of cheating the piss tests – obviously not very successfully. Then I told the court I had organised to do the home detox.

It was a few months before I was to complete the Drug Court program. My urines were coming back dirty too often so my points went up. Once my points went to ten, I needed to bring my points down by spending five days in Bandyup. If I remember rightly I slept for the whole five days.

I got out on Christmas Eve but while I was gone a so-called friend of mine had spoken with my mum and said she was going to take the kids' presents home with her so they didn't get stolen. She actually asked mum to help her load the presents into her car. Sure enough, when I arrived home there were no presents nor could I find my friend anywhere.

I had gone around to her house and she wasn't there. I rang her phone and it was off. I went to her boyfriend's parents' house that night and he told me she had hocked them all.

Between Jerremy and myself we have eleven children of various ages but I knew that eight of our children would be at Christmas lunch the following day, waiting for their presents.

Now this was bad, we had very little money…definitely not enough to buy presents for all the children. And I had wasted the whole day before Christmas looking for this girl.

It was Christmas Day and no presents and the worst thing was the kids knew they were each getting a iPod and a Nintendo DS.

I told Jerremy to take the kids out to see nan and pop and I would meet him out there once I got some presents – I was not rocking up to Christmas with no presents.

Now where was I going to get at least one iPod or a Nintendo DS for each child? I rang a friend, who knew a friend, who knew a friend (so to speak), and got what I could. I then went around to a few shoppers and dealers' houses that I knew, and I arrived at the Christmas lunch at 1p.m. that day with at least one present each. The bigger kids got an iPod and the younger kids got a Nintendo DS.

With the stress and chaos of Christmas I ended up frying myself a bit too much. The following Monday, I missed a reporting, then had another dirty. This resulted in me breaching my Drug Court program.

CHAPTER ELEVEN

# In Prison Again

I was 26 years of age at this point and remanded in Bandyup until a place came up at a rehab somewhere. I didn't see Jer and the kids at all during this time because I didn't want the kids to know I was in prison, so I told them I was fishing on a boat, and I didn't want my man to see me in jail. And I couldn't have handled them coming to visit then leaving without me.

Plus, I didn't want my man to see me in prison clothes and with no make-up on. It's nice to look your best for your man.

This resulted in me being a 'Telstra lady', as I was always on the phone to Jer. As soon as the time limit of ten minutes was finished, I would go to a different phone and call for another ten mins. I have no idea how he didn't get sick of me calling. Sometimes I would call and we had totally run out of things to say, but I still wanted to know he was on the other end of the phone. I believe this started teaching us how to communicate because we didn't have an option to express our feelings in any other way other than talking.

Eight weeks later they notified me that a place had come up at a residential rehabilitation farm south of Perth. I was looking so forward to seeing Jer and the kids on the weekend following my admission.

Once I was there I was shown my room and introduced to everyone. Then it was time to go to the morning group discussion. It is this part of the program that, although I didn't realise it at the time, helped me and Jer get through our communication breakdown in leaps and bounds. This is what saved our relationship and kept us together for the best fourteen years of my life.

In this group everyone had to have a turn of saying how they felt that day. The only words you couldn't say were 'good' or 'bad'. You had to go into detail about how you were feeling without saying those words, and if you try it, it's not quite as easy as you think.

After my first morning at this group therapy, I remember ringing Jerremy and saying, "I hate this place, we have to sit in a group and tell everyone how we feel each day but not use the words good or bad". But the more we did this, the easier it became.

As I was relaying to Jer what I was learning, he was learning as well.

I looked forward to the weekends when Jer and the kids would come to spend the day. I would wait in the smoke shed until I heard a car coming down the street with Akon (my favourite music) being cranked in the car. Then I would run up to greet them.

I missed them all so much – I hadn't seen any of them for two months.

Jer stepped up here, from a man who wasn't even used to looking after himself or the kids because I did it all – he didn't even know where to find his clothes (I would always have them out for him) – he soon learnt to become the best dad. He never left the kids once, he just battled his way through whatever he had to while I was gone.

With the help of the lady in the unit across from our house, he did the washing, maintained the house to the best of his ability, got the kids up in the mornings, showered them all – even learnt to tie up the girl's hair – and got the kids off to kindy and school. He did whatever a dad was supposed to do.

I completed my 12 weeks at Palmerston and Jerremy and the kids never missed one visit.

From this program our violence and fighting became less and less frequent. We had actually made so much progress from learning this one new skill, *communication*. I got out of there to go home, and of course things weren't perfect as we still had our meth addiction, but things were so much better. After five months off everything, I have to say that because I was only in the rehab to beat going to jail, I wasn't ready to get off the gear, and the very first thing I wanted to do, was get on. Jer only had one packet left that he was going to smoke, but he had no chance. I stood over him for the last packet. My using went straight back to the way it was before I went to prison.

Not long after I was released, Jerremy was admitted to hospital for a infection he had on his leg. When they tested his sugar level it was up to 40 and it's only meant to be between 6 and 7. He was diagnosed with diabetes.

I rang him one morning to see how he was feeling and I heard him ask a nurse for a jug of water. When you are a diabetic you get very thirsty when your sugar levels are too high.

It was about four hours later that me and the kids arrived at the hospital, and the second I walked in he said, "can you please get me some water". I couldn't believe he had gone all that time and no one had brought him any water.

I went down immediately and got a jug of water.

After he had drunk it he asked me to get a wheelchair and take him to see whoever was in charge of the ward that day.

Once we got to her office, I knew he would go off but I thought he would have told her what the problem was before the abuse came out. Even I was stunned with what he said but Jer did have a special way with words.

He looked at her and said, "are you in charge here"? She said yes, and Jer went on to say: "You couldn't run a f...k in a brothel with a fist full of fifties...and your nurses, they're not nurses, they're sluts." He was pointing to the ones he had asked for water earlier.

He then said, "come on, let's go home".


We moved up to Butler at the beginning of 2006. It wasn't long before the Clarkson police were smashing down our door looking for money, drugs, implements etc. This ended up being a common occurrence at this house. I think in the six years we were in the Butler house we had around fourteen raids. Some of the raids used to be like you would see on the show, Cops. There used to be police officers coming from every possible angle. After one of the raids was over, and the two demon (undercover) cars, the sniffer dog wagon and the mobile unit left, Jeremy still counted seventeen police officers in our carport. This kind of thing just becomes a common thing in the drug scene.

During the first few raids, the kids used to get terrified.

I remember one time the kids were eating their Weet-Bix at the kitchen table getting ready for school that day. Then next minute the front door was smashed open. The twins were that scared that one of them actually wet their pants, then they hid under the table to watch the police come running from everywhere, shouting for me and Jer to lay on the ground, and they were holding guns to their dad's head, right in front of the children.

Looking back now I have no idea how this lifestyle became our norm, but I wish we were able to see things from a different angle. In our eyes things didn't seem that bad. As we grew up we just learnt to do what you have to do to survive.

Living this way was the only way we knew how to pay for our habits, pay our bills and support our family.

Life continued on the same track until August 12, 2010, it was the day before Jer turned thirty-eight. He got so ill he had eight days off the gear but his body just totally started to shut down. He was battling to breathe, at night I would wake up to hear him choking. Then he would sleep sitting up. One night I woke up because I couldn't hear or feel him in the bed and he was sitting up on the lounge trying to sleep. As the next few days passed his breathing became worse, at times it was as if he just didn't have the strength to take a breath. I kept trying to ask him to go to the doctors but the response was always "no". He was not the sort of man you could make do anything – he either would if he wanted to or wouldn't if he didn't want to. Some days and or nights he would ask me to take him for a drive, just so he could sit in the back of the car with the window down a little bit so the wind could blow into his face, helping him to get air in his lungs.

I finally convinced him to go to the hospital.

Once we got to Joondalup Health Campus Emergency they rushed him straight through as soon as they saw him. His blood pressure was 240/170, he had one-and-a-half to two litres of fluid in his lungs, and he was in a really bad way. He had chronic heart failure.

He was struggling to breathe so much that he asked me to get a piece of cardboard and fan the air into his face to help him breathe.

I thought he was about to go, he thought he was about to go, and the doctors thought he was about to go.

All of a sudden he said, "oi, go and get my pipe and put about a half weight in it and bring it in". (A half weight is about $200 worth of meth)

I got wild and said, "…you can't even breathe and you want your poxy pipe".

He said "just do it, please".

I tried to help him walk to the toilet, which was right next to the nurse's station. He was taking one step, then we would wait for him to catch his breath then he would take another. We were only about half way there and he said, "you go and get it and I'll meet you in the toilets".

I went to the car and melted the gear into the pipe. By the time I had got back he had only made about three steps. I continued to help him to the toilet.

We finally made it. He smoked that whole half a weight and then ripped his drip out and said, "come on, let's go home".

This goes to show how dependent your body can become and how addictive methamphetamine can be.

Having this smoke was enough to get Jer through the night, where without it, because of his addiction of many years, he wouldn't have had a chance.

Four days later he ended up in the Critical Care Unit in Joondalup again.

He was again in a very bad way and we were not sure how he would pull through this one.

One day when his dad was up visiting, Jer had asked if he could change the tube that was supplying the oxygen into his nose to a mask as he wasn't getting enough to breath properly.

One of the nurses must have told a doctor about Jer's addiction and short temper. The doctor changed his tubes to the mask. Then he said, "Jerremy I am going to prescribe you a half a Valium to take the edge off things". Jer ripped off the mask and said, "Renee, tell him". I looked at my father-in-law and smiled.

Then I said to the doctor: "Look, Jer picks up the pipe around 7a.m. in the morning when we get the kids up for school, and the pipe doesn't get put down until bed time, which is usually around 2a.m. in the morning. I don't think that half a Valium is even going to affect him." The doctor's reply stunned me when he said, "that's pretty impressive".

After this they were able to work out Jer's condition and finally understand his moods better.

After about two weeks Jer came home and actually started to get better. We both cut down on the gear but, after what he had been going through, it never actually came to a halt. We were both too afraid to ever go completely off it.

It wasn't long before I started to get sick myself, but mine was a different sickness, I couldn't believe it when I found out I was pregnant. After such a big gap – the twins were eight years old at this stage – out of the blue I was pregnant again. This is something that brought us much closer. About a week before I went into labour I think my hormones went right out of whack. I wanted Jer to go see the lady across the road because our son's motorbike went missing out of her garage. He wouldn't get out of bed so I grabbed a big jug of iced water and threw it all over Jer while he lay there. Well, he flew up, chasing me across the road. I tried to run into the lady's house but the door was locked. He caught me and I was cringing over, trying to block the hit, and he pretended to punch me in the head. He said, "that's it I'm going". He had my car keys. I shouted, "give me my keys", and he said "nope", so, as he tried to pull out I picked up half a brick that was close to my feet and threw it, smashing straight through the passenger window. It just missed his face then smashed through the driver's window. He was wild. He took off, flying around the corner and then after a few minutes he pulled up and said, "oi, get in the car before the police get here". So I jumped in and we didn't come back till the end of the day.

A few days later on November, 10, 2011, Anna Shirley Kennedy was born. Once baby was born Jer and I got so close. Jer doted over baby, she was automatically the boss of our house. During the pregnancy and now after her birth, Anna brought all the family really close. As for Jer and me, we became as one. Our relationship, after starting off so rocky, ended up smooth sailing. We spent all of our days with each other and the children.

I will never fully understand why this bubble burst.

CHAPTER TWELVE

# Confronting My Dad

In March 2013, it was much to my surprise when Jerremy rang me to tell me my dad, Darren, accepted my friend request on Facebook. He ended up writing me a message and asked for my number. I really wanted to speak with him about the unanswered question I had all my life. We spoke that day, but I wasn't going to bring up what I wanted to say on the phone. But in our conversation Darren mentioned he would be coming to Brisbane the following week for two weeks, but then he wouldn't be back in Australia until 2019. Immediately, I thought this is my chance to ask him to his face.

I met Lisa, my biological mother, and spoke with her about what I wanted to do and she said, "if you feel this will help you, I will pay for your airfare and accommodation". All my unanswered questions were about to be answered.

On arrival in Brisbane, Darren met me and Anna at the airport. He looked exactly the same as I remembered. We went down to the undercover parking and we were walking towards a brand new, white Mercedes Benz four-wheel drive. Wow, this was a nice car. We drove for a while and the motorway seemed to go forever. I couldn't believe how much bush surrounded Brisbane. Finally, we turned off the motorway and started to drive up into the hills. This was a pretty area. We got to the top of the road and pulled into this driveway that seemed to be cut into the hill. This was such a nice house, the carport was underneath the house, the garage door lifted up and we pulled into the garage. Inside, there was a lovely Harley Davidson. I commented on how nice it was and he said, "yeh, that's mine, it's a custom designed Harley". We walked up some stairs into the house. I was hoping to see his wife, Jen, and my two half-brothers, Malaki and Jacob, but the house was empty so the boys must have been at school and Jen must have been at work.

Still to this day I think they don't even know they have a half-sister as I never saw them on this trip.

Darren then took me to the hotel; he only came to see me when the boys were at school or at their tutor. I honestly felt I was being hidden away so nobody knew anything about me.

Everything on this trip went wrong, starting from the flight being delayed for four hours, then a really rocky flight. I also broke my ankle while I was waiting for Darren one morning. Then I was so scared to even bring the subject up with Darren as I had no idea how he would respond. On top of that I was in a town where I knew absolutely no one.

It was my last evening in Brisbane and we were in the car on our way to the airport. I had to ask him now as this was the reason I came over in the first place.

I started by saying, "Darren, something came out a few years ago and I want to know your side of the story". He said "what story"? I said "it came out you raped Lisa repeatedly and I am the result of one of these occasions". The way he responded and what he said answered every question I ever had. He said in the most sarcastic way, "nah, it was definitely consensual", then the second I tried to say anything else he cut me short and said very firmly, "drop the subject, I'm not talking about this anymore".

I tried to say, "But I..." He looked at me in the rear vision mirror, with a nasty and horrible look on his face and said sternly, "drop the subject".

If he had said to me he was young and I don't know what got into me or I did something stupid and I am sorry, I would have accepted that.

But with what he said, it showed me I wanted nothing to do with him. He didn't deserve to be in my children's or my life.

After this trip I flew home back to Jer and the kids, and when I told Jer what he had said, Jer said, "don't worry about him, you have got your family here, me and the kids, and we will always love you, no matter what". He was right as always.

I finally had closure on the unfortunate way I was brought into this world. But now it was time to move forward, and to do this I had to let the past go.

I can't change things that happened in the past, no matter how bad it may be but, I can write my own future.

A person's future can be whatever they decide to make it.

CHAPTER THIRTEEN

# Loosing Jer

It was the 3rd of April, 2014, and I was getting the kids off to school. It was Jayde's assembly at Butler Primary School. Jerremy woke up and he was coming down the hallway and he said, "you would want to move, or you're going to miss the assembly". Jer's dad and a very close friend, Steve, were at home with him. I said, "I'm running down now" and off I went.

I had left Anna at home with Jer as she was still asleep on our bed. I watched Jayde's play and then waited to get her attention. I mouthed to her it was a great play and I was heading home as Anna would have been waking soon. She smiled and I left the school.

As I was walking across the oval towards the bottom of our street I looked up and saw two ambulances at the front of our house. I was looking at them and thinking, nah that's not at home but as I got closer, I could see they were both right out the front of our house. I started running so fast I almost tripped over my own legs. Running up that hill, was the longest run of my life, it seemed to take forever.

I finally made it to our house, I ran up the driveway and across the lawn through the front door and down the hallway. As I got into the kitchen I just dropped. In that moment then, my world was ripped apart into tiny little pieces. My world was absolutely shattered when I saw Jer laying there, lifeless on our kitchen floor. I was screaming, "Jer get up, get up", but nothing. I screamed again, "Jer, get up, get up", but nothing. I was trying to shake him and tried to pick his head up to wake him but there was no response.

I started screaming at the ambulance drivers, "why aren't you doing anything"? and they replied, "we have already done everything that we could do". I looked at the clock and it was only 9.05a.m. I had only been gone for twenty minutes. How does someone's world get taken away in twenty minutes?

I knew he was gone but I still tried to wake him for hours. Then, so he wouldn't get cold I asked someone to get him a pillow and a rug and I just lay there with him with my head resting on his shoulder. I will never forget the peacefulness on Jer's face, he was totally out of pain. He actually looked as if he had a smile on his face.

The coroner didn't come until 1p.m. that day. When the coroner's car left our house, our dog, Choppa, got out of the yard and ran right beside the car. The driver had to stop the vehicle so that someone could grab him and bring him back home.

Things went so bad after Jer died, and my house was filled with so many people, some of them total strangers. People were stealing everything they could get their hands on. I had no idea who I could trust or who was there with good intentions or who was there with bad. All I wanted to do was grieve in peace for Jer but people can be so evil in the drug world, and a vulnerable person will always be an easy target, no matter who you are.

I had some of Jer's family members stay with me at different times to help me keep some sort of control over the house and all the people coming through it. I just simply didn't have enough strength to speak let alone ask anyone to leave.

Things were just so confusing due to the grief of Jer's sudden death – the fear of facing the next day and every day after without him. The fear of knowing our family's backbone and protection was now gone, combined with the fear of not knowing who I could trust – on top of the paranoia and scattered thoughts from the drugs – meant my head was in a really bad place.

A few times I wanted to grab the kids and just run, but where do you go when the place you are running from is your own home?

I believe one of the hardest things anyone will ever have to do in life is to organise a loved one's funeral. It's so hard to make all the necessary decisions and choices at a time when you probably wouldn't even be able to spell your own name. We chose a champagne and brass casket, and I organised a Hummer limo to take Jer, as this was the style he deserved. They had to cut bits out of the inside of the Hummer so the casket could fit in.

This day was the hardest day of my life.

There would have been at least a thousand people at Jer's funeral. If you knew Jer you would understand why. He was one of a kind. He always stood up for the underdog, even if he didn't know the person. If someone was getting picked on he would take it up for them and he would start on the person who was doing the bullying. If someone's children were missing out on something he would make sure he got it for them. Sometimes it would be a kid in the neighbourhood who may not have had a scooter. Jer would get a scooter deck that might have been on special somewhere and he would make that boy a darty looking scooter that he could be proud of. All the neighbourhood kids used to come and hang out at our house all day every day and if any of the kids' scooters needed fixing then Jer would spend time with the kids and show them how to fix them. If someone didn't have enough for food for themselves and their family, Jer would make sure I made a massive feed which was enough for the other family as well as ours. Like I said before, Jer was one of a kind. As the words in his funeral song say...he was and still is "The Man".

The day after Jer's funeral things went from bad to worse; his uncle came around to rob me. Thankfully, I wasn't home. Brooke came and picked me and the kids up, and between us we grabbed our most personal belongings, well, what we could fit into our cars. We then based ourselves in Brooke's lounge room for a few months as we were too scared to go home.

This same period the man who Jer used to get on through put a massive amount on top of his bill, which he tried to carry over to me once Jer passed away. He thought I wouldn't be in the right frame of mind to work out what was going on.

As a result of this, I was told two men had come over from Kings Cross with a photo of me, and well, when things like this happen there is not usually a very good outcome.

I went to my sisters to try to get my head around what was going on. After about a week of thinking I worked out a way to find out who this money was supposedly owed to, and I wanted to see them about it. I called Brooke and asked her if she would take me to confront these people and she said, "well I wouldn't let you go alone". Jerremy and I had never run from anyone in our lives, apart from the police, so I wasn't about to start running from a problem like this when I knew it was not true, and I believe a person who runs shows some guilt. I approached them and told them my side of the story and between us we worked out what was going on, and thankfully, it was all sorted out.

After all this I knew I wanted out. I also knew that everything was starting to take a toll on my health.

Brooke helped me move away from Perth to start afresh. Not long after we moved down south, I was on facebook one day and I saw a post about a celebrity medium that was coming to Perth on a tour the following week. I rang up thankfully he had a couple of places left so I made a booking to see him while he was here.

I drove up to Perth and when I arrived at the hotel and met him he was a really cool down to earth guy. For much of the reading he was communicating with Jerremy, who said he was needing to pass on a vital message to me, that if I didn't get off the drugs soon, then I too was going to also pass away. I felt such emotion and a huge sense of relief washed over me knowing that Jerremy was still around, still by my side. Before I left that day he made me promise that as soon as I left I would call an organisation near my home and make an appointment to start the process of recovery. He also wanted me to call him and let him know when the appointment was made.

I left there that day, and my head was going frantic. I knew in my heart that everything he said was true. But hearing these words hit a massive trigger inside of me.

If I were to die then what would happen to my children? Who would be there to love them, to care for them, to keep them safe, to help them make the right choices in life, to be there at all the important events throughout their lives.....

I made a decision that day and it was the most important decision of my life.... No way was I going anywhere..... I will be here for my children for as long as I possibly can and I will do whatever I needed to do to make sure it happens....

I cut my daily using down to a minimum, but was so scared of how I was going to be able to go through with the final step. I knew it was going to be so hard without any help. I went to see a local doctor. I was so ashamed because I had never voluntarily spoken with anybody about my addiction at all, but I had to put my pride aside, so I did. I told him I had an eighteen-year methamphetamine addiction and I had cut my usage down, but I needed help with the last step. When I looked up, the doctor was already on the Department of Child Protection website, he was about to report me. My heart sunk. I left the practice that day crying my eyes out. How can someone go to seek help and the doctor acts in this way? But I wasn't going to let him stop me from my recovery; I just had to find another way.

I spoke with my sister Olivia, and told her I was planning to get off altogether. She had arranged with a few ladies from church to make a whole heap of meals for me and the kids, and my sister and her husband were going to help me get the kids ready and off to school and I would sleep and go through the withdrawal at home. This plan seemed like it would work, but my kids didn't even know I used so I didn't want them to see me doing a detox.

I ended up finding a place in Queensland where I stayed for ten days. It was no rehab or anything like that but it was a place where my kids didn't have to see me going through the big crash, and I didn't know a soul, so I couldn't just go and get on when the detox got too hard.

I had my last taste on the way to Perth Airport. This would be my last day on drugs – it was the 7$^{th}$ of November, 2014.

I flew over and stayed on a farm and did an unsupervised detox, even though now I realise how dangerous this was after an addiction of so many years. But apart from when I was in prison and rehab, this was the first time I had ever been without the gear, ever.

The first few days it was the big crash, I tried to take some Valium but it smashed me too much so I didn't take them after the second day. My body was totally and utterly aching. The dizziness is overpowering, every time I stood up I felt as if I was about to topple over. As for the third and fourth day, I am so sorry to my best friend, Brooke…what can I say other than that she did cop the lot.

Even though it was my idea about going over to Queensland, I remember calling her and screaming my head off. I reckon if I had looked in a mirror at this time I would have had steam coming out of my ears, nose and any outlet possible, I was that angry.

So the other people didn't hear me, I tried to take my phone out to the road when I called her, but I must have forgotten other people might hear because I really flew off the handle. One of the staff members who lived at a neighbouring property heard the yelling, and when she looked out onto the road to see who was screaming, she couldn't believe it was me. The other people who were staying in the same house were too scared to even come outside to see if I was OK. They just hid in their rooms.

These anger outbursts and paranoid thoughts carried on for a few days until I spoke to my kids, and a few of them were having a really hard time without me being at home with them. It was then I remembered the reason I was doing all of this.

This is where my change of thinking started. If I could do this long off the gear out of jail and where it was fully my own choice, and off my own back well, I wasn't going to waste it. If I can go this long, then I can keep going. I need to be here for my children.

When I arrived back in Perth, the second any thought of getting on crossed my mind, I looked at a photo of Jer and I said, "come on, kids in the car we are going home". I removed myself from any place that I would have been weakened.

So many people were having so much to say, and there were so many yarns going around about me and why I moved away. Of course, some of this hurt as a lot was being said by people who I really cared about. I would realise that none of that matters. I needed to focus on making the necessary changes to get myself and the kids through the grief and continue my recovery.

I stayed away from Perth and disconnected myself from anyone I knew, to keep away from anything that may have instigated a relapse.

The only way for me to have a totally successful recovery after an addiction to risky behaviours and a massive methamphetamine addiction of so many years, is to concentrate on a total fresh start. New environment, new friends. A whole new daily routine.

People going through struggles like these need encouragement and support.

Negative behaviours and patterns need to be exchanged with positive ones. So I kept myself as busy as possible to keep my mind active and keep moving forward. This also ensured that boredom didn't get the better of me because I believe if I was sitting around at home doing nothing, I may have had more thoughts or cravings about getting back on. There was no way in the world I was going to let that happen.

I went around to a few organisations in the Bunbury area, to apply for volunteer work, but this was a hard one with a criminal record and without the right credentials. I had a Certificate III in Secretarial and Administration from 1996 but this was way out of date and the Certificate III in Community Services that I started when I was in Nyandi Prison in 2008 was incomplete.

One of the organisations I did approach about a volunteer position working with women going through domestic violence had said to me they could only give me a position if I had completed a Certificate IV in Community Services.

That very day I rang up the South West Institute of Technology and spoke with the lecturers. I was honest from the very start with them about my past and my desire to use my past to help others who may be going through similar struggles in their lives. They were immediately supportive of my intentions. We then started the process of getting enrolled. The following Wednesday I commenced Certificate IV in Community Services.

Doing this course helped me in so many ways – along with working in the professional community services field – it helped me grow on a personal level. It also helped me identify the impact our lifestyle might have on our children and how to respond if any issues should arise. It also helped me realise healthy lifestyle and the boundaries of a family, and helped the kids and I grow together as a family and be there for each other through the stages of the grief process.

Not long after I stated the course I started hearing a weird voice in my head. Thoughts about going to church and discovering my spiritual side kept nagging at me, I kept feeling that I needed to call my sister Olivia, to find out what time church was on. When I finally got hold of her she was in shock! She couldn't believe I wanted to know what time church was on off my own back! She happily told me it was at 10 am on Sunday. She came over at 9.30 am that Sunday, I followed her there and by 10 am I was sitting in the church. No one was more surprised than me. What was more amazing was that the pastor was talking about changing lives and transforming communities! I had no idea that churches were so interested in helping people with drug problems and domestic violence problems. I never thought about what they did in churches. I never thought I would end up in one. Me and Olivia just looked at each other and smiled. I knew I had made the right decision.

On July 24, 2015, after a lot of perseverance and the support from my sister Olivia, her wonderful family, a close friend and the encouragement and patience of the lecturers, I passed the course.

I had started taking my kids to church in Bunbury, and at first I felt a little unsure, not knowing what to expect, because of the life I had lived but I found God and believe it or not a month before I completed my Certificate IV, I was baptized.

I do thank you Jesus for not giving up on me. I do believe that God has had His hand on my shoulder keeping me safe all these years, but I just didn't realize it, and because of His love support and guidance I have come out of this, on the other side of life.

Life now has no limits…

On Wednesday, the 9$^{th}$ of September, 2015, I completed and passed a Diploma in Nutritional Therapy.

And on the 16$^{th}$ of October, 2015, I received notification I passed the Diploma in Mindfulness Based Cognitive Behavioural Therapy.

This story is just the beginning.

## Acknowledgments

Jesus Christ, my Lord and my Saviour, I thank you for straightening my windy road, so that I could find a new direction in life. I do believe that you have had your hand on my shoulder keeping me safe all these years, but I just didn't realise it.

I want to thank my best friend and the love of my life, Jerremy…you truly are my inspiration. I thank you for teaching me how to love and be happy with life. We may have had a bumpy start, but getting through it just made us stronger.

We grew through every situation we were faced with.

In the end we did become as one.

I will love you always.

I want to thank all 11 of our children, who have never been anything but supportive and an inspiration to me.

The loving and unconditional support of my family and friends was an important part of my journey and in the writing of this book.

Thank you to my beautiful mother who never gave up on me. She always tried to accept and understand my actions and life no matter how outrageous they may have been.

My beautiful mother-in-law, who has been a supportive role model to me over the years since I met Jerremy.

To my awesome friends, thank you for being the supportive network that I needed to be able to get through my grief and recovery and now turn my life around.

A special thank you to Brooke, Dom and their wonderful children, who have been there for so many years through thick and thin. You were there for me in the hardest time of my life, losing Jerremy, and every event after. I cannot even describe how much your friendship means to me and the kids. I thank you.

A special thank you to my beautiful sister, Olivia, and her wonderful family, her husband Byron, and the boys. I thank you for your unconditional love, support and guidance. Olivia, you have always been like a second mother to me, you also never gave up on me. Your belief in me has been such an inspiration. I thank you.

A special thank you to my good friend Crissy and her son, for your friendship and support over the years. For helping me adjust to a new way of life, I thank you.

www.ingramcontent.com/pod-product-compliance
Lightning Source LLC
Chambersburg PA
CBHW040329300426
44113CB00020B/2705